POWERFUL FAITH

POWERFUL FAITH

R.A. TORREY

Whitaker House

Unless otherwise indicated, all Scripture quotations are from the *King James Version* (KJV) of the Bible.

Scripture quotations marked (RV) are taken from the *Revised Version* of the Holy Bible.

POWERFUL FAITH

ISBN: 0-88368-417-9
Printed in the United States of America
Copyright © 1996 by Whitaker House

Whitaker House
580 Pittsburgh Street
Springdale, PA 15144

1 2 3 4 5 6 7 8 9 10 11 / 06 05 04 03 02 01 00 99 98 97 96

Contents

1

The Testimony of Jesus Christ

The most important question in religious thought is, "Is the Bible the Word of God?" If the Bible is the Word of God, if it is an absolutely trustworthy revelation of God and man and eternal realities, then we have a starting point from which we can proceed and conquer the whole domain of religious truth. But, if the Bible is not the Word of God, if it is the mere product of man's thinking, speculating, and guessing, if it is not altogether trustworthy in regard to religious and eternal truth, then we are all at sea, not knowing where we are drifting, but we may be sure that we are not drifting toward any safe port.

I did not always believe the Bible to be the Word of God. At one time I sincerely doubted that it was. I doubted that Jesus Christ was the Son of God. I doubted that there was a personal God. I was not an infidel—I was a skeptic. I did not deny—I questioned. I was not an atheist—I was an agnostic. I did not know, but I determined to find out. If there was a God, I determined to find that out and act accordingly. If Jesus Christ was the Son of God, I determined to find that out and act accordingly. If the Bible was the Word of God, I determined to find that out and act accordingly.

I found out. I found out beyond any doubt that there is a God, that Jesus Christ is the Son of God, and that the Bible is the Word of God. Today, I do not consider these things to be a matter of mere probability, nor even of mere belief, but of absolute certainty.

I am going to give you some of the reasons why I believe the Bible to be the Word of God. I will not give you all the reasons—it would take months to do that. I will not even give you the reasons that are most conclusive to me personally, for these are of such a personal and experimental nature that they cannot be conveyed to another. But I will give you reasons that will prove conclusive to any sincere seeker after the truth, to anyone who desires to know the truth and is willing to obey it. They will not convince one who is determined not to know the truth, or who is unwilling to obey it. If one will not receive the love of the truth, he must be left to his own deliberate choice of error, and he must be given over to strong delusion to believe a lie (2 Thess. 2:11). But, if one is searching for the truth, no matter how completely he is in the fog today, he can be led into the truth.

I believe the Bible to be the Word of God, first of all, because of the testimony of Jesus Christ to that fact. We live in a day in which many men say that they accept the teaching of Jesus Christ, but that they do not accept the teaching of the whole Bible. They say that they believe what Jesus said, but as for what Moses said, or is said to have said, and what Isaiah said, or is said to have said, and what Jeremiah said, and Paul said, and John said, and what the rest of the Bible writers said, they do not know about that.

This position may at first glance seem rational, but, in fact, it is utterly irrational. If we accept the teaching of Jesus Christ, we must accept the whole Bible, for Jesus Christ has put the stamp of His authority on the entire Book. And if we accept His authority, we must accept everything on which He puts the stamp of His authority.

CHRIST'S ENDORSEMENT OF THE OLD TESTAMENT

As for Christ's endorsement of the Old Testament, look first of all at Mark 7:10–13. He is speaking here to the Pharisees and scribes:

> *For Moses said, Honour thy father and thy mother; and, Whoso curseth father or mother, let him die the death: but ye say, If a man shall say to his father or mother, It is Corban, that is to say, a gift, by whatsoever thou mightest be profited by me; he shall be free. And ye suffer him no more to do ought for his father or his mother; making the word of God of none effect through your tradition, which ye have delivered: and many such like things do ye.*

In these verses, Jesus begins by quoting from the Ten Commandments, as well as from another portion of the Law of Moses. (See Exodus 20:12; 21:17.) Then He compares the teaching of the Law of Moses to the traditions of the Pharisees and scribes. Then He says, "You make '*the word of God* of none effect through your tradition' (v. 13, italics added)." Here He distinctly calls the Law of Moses the "word of God."

It is oftentimes said that the Bible nowhere claims to be the Word of God. Here Jesus Christ Himself distinctly asserts that the Law of Moses is the Word of God. If, then, we accept the authority of Jesus Christ, we must accept the Law of Moses as the Word of God. Of course, this only covers the first five books of the Old Testament, but if we can accept this as the Word of God, we will have little difficulty with the rest of the Old Testament, for it is here that the hottest battle is being fought today.

Look at Matthew 5:18. Here Jesus says, "Till heaven and earth pass, one jot or one tittle shall in no wise pass from the law, till all be fulfilled." Now every Hebrew scholar knows that a "jot" is the Hebrew character *yodh,* the smallest character in the Hebrew alphabet, less than half the size of any other character. And, he knows that a "tittle" is a little horn that the Hebrews put on their consonants. Here Jesus asserts that the Law of Moses, as originally given, is absolutely infallible down to its smallest letter and part of a letter. If, then, we accept the authority of Jesus Christ, we must accept the authority of the Law of Moses as originally given and as contained in the Old Testament Scriptures.

Look now at John 10:34–35:

> *Jesus answered them, Is it not written in
> your law, I said, Ye are gods?...He
> called them gods, unto whom the word
> of God came, and the scripture cannot be
> broken.*

Jesus has just quoted from Psalms 82:6, and
then He adds, "The scripture cannot be broken." Thus, He puts the stamp of His authority on the absolute inerrancy of the Old
Testament Scriptures.

Read Luke 24:27, and note the words *in all
the scriptures*: "Beginning at Moses and all the
prophets, he expounded unto them in all the
scriptures the things concerning himself." And
in verse forty-four He says, "All things must be
fulfilled, which were written in the law of
Moses, and in the prophets, and in the
psalms."

Now every scholar knows that the Jews di-
vided their Bible (our present Old Testament)
into three parts: the law (the first five books of
the Old Testament), the prophets (most of the
books that we call prophetic and some of those
that we call historical), and the psalms or sacred
writings (the remaining books of the Old Testament). Jesus Christ takes each one of these
three recognized divisions of the Old Testament
and puts the stamp of His authority on each of

them. If, then, we accept the authority of Jesus Christ, we are logically driven to accept the entire Old Testament.

In Luke 16:31 Jesus says, "If they hear not Moses and the prophets, neither will they be persuaded, though one rose from the dead," thus in the most emphatic way endorsing the truth of the Old Testament Scriptures.

In John 5:47 He says, "If ye believe not his [Moses'] writings, how shall ye believe my words?" Thus, He puts the stamp of His authority on the teaching of Moses. He is saying that the teaching of Moses is as truly from God as His own.

CHRIST'S ENDORSEMENT OF THE NEW TESTAMENT

We must then, if we accept the authority of Jesus Christ, accept the entire Old Testament. But what about the New Testament? Did Jesus put the stamp of His authority on it also? He did. But how could He when not one book of the New Testament had been written when He left this earth? By way of anticipation. Look at John 14:26, and see what Jesus says:

The Comforter, which is the Holy Ghost, whom the Father will send in my name,

> *he shall teach you all things, and bring*
> *all things to your remembrance, whatso-*
> *ever I have said unto you.*

Thus, He puts the stamp of His authority, not only on the apostolic teaching as given by the Holy Spirit, but on the apostolic recollection of what He Himself had taught.

The question is often asked, "How do we know that the gospel records are an accurate reproduction of the teachings of Jesus Christ?" It is asked, "Did the apostles take notes at the time of what Jesus said?" There is reason to believe that they did, that Matthew and Peter (from whom Mark derived his material) and James (from whom, there is reason to believe, Luke obtained much of his material) took notes of what Jesus said in Aramaic, and that John took notes of what Jesus said in Greek, and that we have in the four gospels the report of what they took down at the time.

However, whether this is true or not does not matter for our present purposes, for we have Christ's own statement that the apostolic records are not the apostles' recollection of what Jesus said, but the Holy Spirit's recollection of what Jesus said. While the apostles might forget and report inaccurately, the Holy Spirit could not forget.

Furthermore, look at John 16:12–13, and see what Jesus says:

I have yet many things to say unto you, but ye cannot bear them now. Howbeit when he, the Spirit of truth, is come, he will guide you into all truth.

Here Jesus puts the stamp of His authority on the teaching of the apostles. He says that their teaching is given by the Holy Spirit, contains all the truth, and contains truth in addition to His own teaching. He tells the apostles that He has many things to tell them that they are not yet ready to receive, but that when the Holy Spirit comes, He will guide them into this fuller and larger truth. If, then, we accept the authority of Jesus Christ, we must accept the apostolic teaching (the New Testament writings) as being given through the Holy Spirit, as containing all the truth, and as containing more truth than Jesus taught while on earth.

There are many in our day crying, "Back to Christ," by which they usually mean, "We do not care what Paul taught, what John taught, what James taught, or what Jude taught. We do not know about them. Let us go back to Christ, the original source of authority, and accept what He taught, and that alone."

Very well, "Back to Christ." The cry is not a bad one, for when you get back to Christ, you hear Christ Himself saying, "On to the apostles. They have more truth to teach than I have taught. The Holy Spirit has taught them all the truth. Listen to them." If, then, we accept the authority of Jesus Christ, we are driven to accept the authority of the entire New Testament.

So, then, if we accept the teaching of Jesus Christ, we must accept the entire Old Testament and the entire New Testament. It is either Christ and the whole Bible, or no Christ and no Bible. There are some people these days who say that they believe in Christ, but not in the Christ of the New Testament. But, there is no Christ except the Christ of the New Testament. Any other Christ than the Christ of the New Testament is a pure figment of the imagination. Any other Christ than the Christ of the New Testament is an idol made by man's own fancy, and whoever worships him is an idolater.

FIVE DIVINE TESTIMONIES TO JESUS' AUTHORITY

We must accept the authority of Jesus Christ. He is commended to us by five unmistakable divine testimonies.

The Divine Life That Jesus Lived

First is the testimony of the divine life that He lived, for He lived as no other man ever lived. Let any man take the four gospels and read them carefully and candidly; he will soon be convinced of two things. First, he will be convinced that he is reading the story of a life actually lived. No man could have imagined the character there set forth. Much less could four men have imagined a character, each one making his own account of that character consistent, not only with itself, but with the other three. To suppose that the four writers of the Gospels imagined Jesus' life would be to suppose a greater miracle than any recorded in the Gospels.

The candid reader will be convinced, secondly, that the life here set forth is separate from all other human lives, that it stands by itself, that it is clearly a divine life lived under human conditions. Napoleon Bonaparte was a good judge of men. He once said, regarding the life of Jesus Christ as recorded in the Gospels, which he had been reading, "I know men [and if he did not know men, who ever did?], and Jesus Christ was not a man." What he meant was, of course, that Jesus Christ was not a mere man.

The Divine Words That He Spoke

Jesus Christ is commended to us by a second unmistakable divine testimony. It is the divine words that He spoke. If anyone will study the teachings of Jesus Christ with openness and faithfulness, he will soon see that they have a character that distinguishes them from all other teachings ever uttered on earth.

The Divine Works That He Did

Third, Jesus Christ was commended to us by the divine works that He did, not only healing the sick, which many others have done, but cleansing the leper, opening the eyes of the blind, raising the dead (see Matthew 11:4–5), stilling the tempest by a word (see Mark 4:37–39), turning water into wine (see John 2:1–10), and feeding five thousand with five small loaves and two small fishes (see Matthew 14:16–21). These miracles of power are clear credentials of a God-sent teacher. We cannot study them candidly and not come to the same conclusion as Nicodemus did: "We know that thou art a teacher come from God: for no man can do these miracles that thou doest, except God be with him" (John 3:2).

Of course, strenuous efforts have been made to eliminate the supernatural element from the story of the life of Jesus Christ, but all these efforts have resulted in failure, and all similar efforts must result in failure. The most able effort of this kind was that of David Strauss in his *Leben Jesu*. David Strauss was a man of remarkable ability and gifts, a man of real and profound scholarship, a man of notable genius, a man of singular power in critical analysis, a man of indomitable perseverance and untiring industry. He applied all the rare gifts of his richly endowed mind to a study of the story of Jesus' life, with the determination to discredit its miraculous element. He spent his best years and strength in this effort.

If anyone could have succeeded in such an effort, David Strauss was the man, but he failed utterly. For a time it seemed to many that he had succeeded in his purpose, but when his study of Jesus was itself submitted to rigid, critical analysis, it fell to pieces, and to-day is utterly discredited. In fact, others who wish to eliminate the miraculous element from the story of Jesus feel that they must make the attempt anew, since the attempt of David Strauss has come to nothing.

Where David Strauss failed, Ernest Renan tried again. He had not, by any means, the ability and mind of Strauss, but he was a man of brilliant genius, of subtle imagination, of rare literary skill, and of singular finesse. His *Life of Jesus* was read with interest and admiration by many. The work was done with fascinating skill. Some fancied that Ernest Renan had succeeded in his attempt, but his *Life of Jesus* was discredited in an even shorter time than David Strauss's work.

All other attempts have met with a similar fate. It is an attempt at the impossible. Let any objective man take the life of Jesus and read it for himself with attention and care, and he will soon discover that the life there pictured could not have been imagined. He will see that Jesus' teachings are not fictitious teachings put into the mouth of a fictitious person, but they are the real utterances of a real person. He will also discover that the character and the teaching set forth in the Gospels, are inextricably interwoven with the stories of the miracles. He will find that if you eliminate the miracles, the character and the teaching disappear. The character and the teachings cannot be separated from the miraculous element without a violence that no reasonable man will permit.

Today, this much at least is proven, that Jesus lived and did precisely as it is recorded in the four gospels. Personally, I believe that more than this is proven, but this is enough for our present purpose. If Jesus lived and did precisely as the Gospels record—cleansing the lepers, opening the eyes of the blind, raising the dead, stilling the tempest with His word, feeding the five thousand with the five small loaves and the two small fishes—then He bears unmistakable credentials as a teacher sent and endorsed by God.

His Divine Influence on History

Fourth, Jesus Christ is also commended to us by His divine influence on all subsequent history. Jesus Christ was definitely one of three things: He was either the son of God in a unique sense (a divine person incarnate in human form), or else He was the most daring impostor that ever lived, or else He was one of the most hopeless lunatics. There can be no honest doubt about Jesus' claims: He claimed that He was the Son of God in a unique sense (John 5:17–18), that all men should honor Him even as they honor the Father (John 5:23), that He and the Father were one (John 10:30), and that whoever had seen Him had seen the Father (John 14:9).

So, He was either the divine Person that He claimed to be, or the most daring impostor, or a most hopeless lunatic. Was His influence on

subsequent history the influence of a lunatic?
No one but a lunatic would say so. Was His influence on subsequent history the influence of
an impostor? No one except a person whose own
heart is thoroughly corrupted by deceit and
fraud would ever think of saying so. He was not
an impostor or a lunatic. We have only one al-
ternative left: He was what He claimed to be—
the Son of God.

His Resurrection from the Dead

Fifth, Jesus Christ is commended to us by
His resurrection from the dead. Later on I will
present the evidence for the resurrection of
Jesus Christ. We will see that the historical
evidence for the resurrection of Christ is absolutely convincing in its character, that the
resurrection of Jesus Christ from the dead is
one of the best-proven facts of history.

The resurrection of Christ is God's seal to
Christ's claim. Jesus Christ claimed to be the
Son of God. He was put to death for making
that claim. Before being put to death, He said
that God would set His seal to the claim by
raising Him from the dead. (See Mark 8:31.)
They killed Him; they laid Him in the sepulcher; they rolled a stone to the door of the sepulcher; they sealed that door with the Roman

seal (Matt. 27:65–66), which to break was death. When the appointed hour of which Christ had spoken came, the breath of God swept through His dead body, and Jesus rose triumphant over death. In this, God spoke more clearly than if He would speak from the open heavens today and say, "This is my beloved Son: hear him" (Mark 9:7).

We must then, if we are honest, accept the authority of Jesus Christ. But, as already seen, if we accept the authority of Jesus Christ, we must accept the entire Old Testament and the entire New Testament as being the Word of God. Therefore, I believe the Bible to be the Word of God because of the testimony of Jesus Christ to that effect.

JESUS VERSUS THE SCHOOL OF CRITICISM

A school of criticism has arisen that presumes to set up its authority in place of the authority of Jesus Christ. They say, for example, "Jesus said that Psalm 110 was by David and was Messianic (see Matthew 22:42–45), but we say that Psalm 110 is neither by David nor is Messianic." They ask us to give up the authority and infallibility of Jesus Christ and the Bible, and to accept their authority and their infallibility instead. Very well, but before doing it, we demand their credentials. We do not yield to anyone's claim of authority and infallibility until he presents his credentials.

Jesus Christ presents His credentials. First of all, He presents the credential of the divine life that He lived. What do they have to compare with that? We hear much about the beautiful lives of some men in this school of critics. We have no desire to deny the claim, but against the beauty of their lives we put the life of Jesus. Which suffers by the comparison? If there is any truth in the argument, "If a man's life is in the right, his doctrine cannot be in the wrong"—and there is truth in the argument—it testifies immeasurably more for the authority of Jesus Christ than it does for the authority of any critic or school of critics.

Second, Jesus presents the credential of the divine words that He spoke. What do they have to compare with that? The words of Jesus Christ have stood the test of century after century, and they shine out with luster and glory today more than ever. What school of criticism has ever stood the test of even twenty years? If one has to choose between the teaching of Christ and that of any school of criticism, it will not take any sane man long to choose.

Third, Jesus Christ presents His third credential, the divine works that He did. They are the unmistakable seal of God on His claims. What does this school of criticism have to compare with that? Absolutely nothing. It has no miracles but miracles of literary ingenuity in the attempt to make the preposterous appear historical.

Fourth, Jesus Christ presents the credential of His influence on human history. We all know what the influence of Jesus Christ has been, how favorable and how divine. Everything that is best in modern civilization, everything that is best in national, domestic, and individual life, is due to the influence of Jesus Christ. Alas! We also know the influence of this school of criticism. We know that it is weakening the power of ministers and Christian workers everywhere. We know that it is emptying churches. We know that it is depleting missionary treasuries. We know that it is paralyzing missionary effort in every field where it has gone. I know this by personal observation and not by hearsay. This may not be their intention. With some of them it is not their intention, but nonetheless it is a fact. The influence of Jesus has been thoroughly beneficial. The influence of this school of criticism has been utterly bad.

Jesus presents His fifth credential, His resurrection from the dead. What does this school of criticism have to compare with that? Nothing whatsoever. Jesus Christ establishes His claim. The opposing school of criticism stands speechless.

Therefore, we refuse to bow to the assumed and unsubstantiated authority and infallibility of any school of criticism, of any priest, of any pope, or of any theological professor, but most gladly do we bow to the authority and infallibility of Jesus Christ, so completely proven. Upon His authority we accept the entire Old Testament and the entire New Testament as the Word of God.

2

Bible Prophecies Fulfilled

In the last chapter, we saw that if we accept the authority of Jesus Christ, we must accept the entire Old Testament and the entire New Testament, because He put the stamp of His authority on both. We saw that it was either Christ and the whole Bible, or no Christ and no Bible. We saw, also, that we must accept the authority of Jesus Christ because He was commended to us by five unmistakably divine testimonies: first, the testimony of the divine life that He lived; second, the testimony of the divine words that He spoke; third, the testimony of the divine works that He did; fourth, the testimony of His divine influence on all subsequent history; and fifth, the testimony of His resurrection from the dead.

We saw, in the next place, that there was a school of criticism that presumed to set up its authority against that of Jesus Christ. This school of criticism demanded that we give up the infallibility of Christ and the Scriptures and instead accept this school of criticism as infallible. Before yielding to their demand, we demanded their credentials. We saw that Jesus presented His credentials, which were convincing, but that this school of criticism had absolutely no credentials to compare with those of Jesus. Therefore, we refused to bow to their claim of authority and infallibility, but we most gladly bowed to the fully proven authority and infallibility of Jesus Christ.

THE BIBLE'S FULFILLED PROPHECIES

Now I would like to move on in my list of reasons why I believe the Bible to be the Word of God. My second reason is the Bible's fulfilled prophecies. The average unbeliever knows absolutely nothing about fulfilled prophecy, and this is not surprising, for the average Christian knows nothing about fulfilled prophecy. Even the average preacher knows practically nothing about fulfilled prophecy. The subject of prophecy is a large one, and to go into it thoroughly would take many chapters. But it can be presented in outline form in a few pages with sufficient fullness to show the overwhelming weight of the argument. There are two kinds of prophecy in the Bible: first, the explicit verbal prophecies; and second, the prophecies of the types and symbols.

Verbal Prophecies

We will first examine the explicit verbal prophecies. There are three kinds: first, prophecies regarding the coming Messiah; second, prophecies regarding the Jewish people; and third, prophecies regarding the Gentile nations. We will limit this discussion to prophecies regarding the coming Messiah, and I ask you to take the time to read five of them by way of illustration: Isaiah 53 (the entire chapter), Micah 5:2, Daniel 9:25–27, Jeremiah 23:5–6, and Psalm 16:8–11.

These passages are predictions of the coming King of Israel. We are told the exact time of His manifestation to His people, the exact place of His birth, the family of which He would be born, and the condition of the family at the time of His birth (a condition entirely different from that existing at the time the prophecy was written, and contrary to all the probabilities in the case). We are also told the manner of His reception by His people (a reception entirely different from that which would naturally be expected), and the specific circumstances regarding His death, His burial, His resurrection, and His victory subsequent to His resurrection. These predictions were fulfilled with the most minute precision in Jesus of Nazareth.

The rationalists have attempted to show that Isaiah 53 does not refer to the coming Messiah. It is natural that they should attempt this, for if it does refer to the coming Messiah, the case of the rationalists is hopeless. That it does refer to the coming Messiah is evident from the fact that this chapter was taken to be Messianic by the Jews themselves until its fulfillment in Jesus of Nazareth, and their unwillingness to accept Him as the Messiah drove them into the attempt to show that it was not Messianic.

Furthermore, the desperate straits to which those who deny its Messianic application are driven, show the hopelessness of their case. When asked who the suffering one of Isaiah 53 is, if he is not the Messiah, the best answer they can give is that it refers to suffering Israel. But anyone who will carefully read the passage will see that this interpretation is impossible. The sufferer of Isaiah 53 is represented as suffering for the sins of people other than himself, and those for whom he is suffering are represented as "my people" (v. 8), that is, Israel. Now, if the sufferer is suffering for sins of people other than himself, and the others for whom he is suffering are Israel, then surely the sufferer himself cannot be Israel.

You can bring these five prophecies down to the very latest date to which the most daring critic ever thought of assigning them, and still they are hundreds of years before the birth of Jesus of Nazareth. How are we going to account for the fact that this Book has the power of looking hundreds of years into the future and predicting with most minute precision things to come, and that these predictions are fulfilled to the very letter? Facts demand accounting for. Theologians may weave their theories out of their own inner consciousness without regard to facts; but logical thinkers must face facts, and here are facts. There is only one rational explanation for it. Any book that has the power of looking hundreds of years into the future and predicting with minute precision the person, place, time, circumstances, and details of things to occur, must have for its author the only person in the universe who knows the end from the beginning— that is, God.

Of course, it is quite possible for a farseeing man to look a few years into the future and, by studying causes now operant, predict in a general way some things that will occur. But this is not at all the case with the Bible. It is not a few years into the future, but hundreds of years into the future; it is not in a general way, but with minute and specific fullness. The Bible did not predict things of which the causes could be discerned at the time, but things that seemed unlikely to be fulfilled but were fulfilled to the letter. To a mind willing to bow to facts and their necessary meaning, these fulfilled prophecies are conclusive evidence of the divine origin of the Book.

A noteworthy fact regarding the prophecies of the Bible is that oftentimes there are two seemingly contradictory lines of prophecy, and it seems that if the one line of prophecy were fulfilled, the other could not be. Yet, these two seemingly contradictory lines of prophecy converge and are fulfilled in one person. For example, in the Old Testament we have two lines of prophecy concerning the Messiah. One line predicts a suffering Messiah, "despised and rejected of men; a man of sorrows, and acquainted with grief" (Isa. 53:3), whose earthly mission would end in death and ignominy. The other line of prophecy predicts, with equal clearness and definiteness, an all-conquering Messiah, who would rule the nations with "a rod of iron" (Ps. 2:9).

How can both of these lines of prophecy be true? The best answer the ancient Jew had, before the fulfillment of both lines in Christ, was that there were to be two Messiahs, one a suffering Messiah of the tribe of Joseph, and one a conquering Messiah of the tribe of Judah. But in the actual fulfillment, both lines of prophecy meet in the one Person, Jesus of Nazareth. At His first coming, He is the suffering Messiah, making atonement for sin by His death upon the cross, as so often predicted in the Old Testament. At His second coming, He is a conquering King to rule the nations. (See Revelation 11:15.)

Prophecies of the Types and Symbols

The prophecies of the types and symbols are even more conclusive than the explicit verbal prophecies. If you ask the ordinary, superficial student of the Bible, how much of the Old Testament is prophetical, he will reply something like this: "Isaiah, Jeremiah, Ezekiel, Daniel, and the Minor Prophets are prophetical," and he may add that there are also prophetical passages here and there in the Psalms and Pentateuch. But if you ask an earnest student of the Bible how much of the Old Testament is prophetical, he will tell you that the entire book is prophetical, that its history is prophetical, that its personages are prophetical, that its institutions, ceremonies, offerings, and feasts are prophetical.

If you are incredulous at his reply (as you have a right to be until you have investigated), but will take the time, he will sit down with you and take you through the whole Old Testament from the first chapter of Genesis to the last chapter of Malachi, and he will show you everywhere unmistakable foreshadowings of things to come! He will show you in the lives of Abraham, Isaac, Joseph, David, and Solomon unquestionable foreshadowings of the truth regarding Christ. He will show you in every sacrifice and offering, in every feast, in every institution, in the tabernacle, in every part of the tabernacle—its outer court, Holy Place, Most Holy Place, brazen altar, golden candlestick, table of showbread, golden altar of incense, ark of the covenant, the veil that hung between the Holy Place and Most Holy Place, in its boards, bars, sockets, and the very coverings of the tabernacle—the clearest setting forth of every truth about Christ. These things speak of His person, His nature, His character, His atoning death,

His resurrection, His ascension, His coming again, and all the facts of Jewish and Christian history. He will show you every profound truth that was to be fully revealed in the New Testament, prefigured in the types and symbols of the Old Testament.

At first, this will very likely seem to you like a mere coincidence, but as you go on verse after verse, chapter after chapter, book after book, if you are a fair-minded man, you will at last be overwhelmingly convinced that this was the thought and intention of the real author. As you see in the Old Testament the setting forth of all the profound truths of Christian doctrine and the perfect foreshadowing of all the facts of the history of Christ, the Jewish people, and the church, you will be driven to recognize in it the mind and wisdom of God. The modern critical theories regarding the authorship of Exodus, Leviticus, Numbers, and Deuteronomy go to pieces when considered in the light of the meaning of the types of the Old Testament. I have never known a destructive critic who knew anything to speak of regarding the types. One cannot study them thoroughly without being profoundly convinced that the real author of the Old Testament, behind the human authors, is God.

THE UNITY OF THE BIBLE

My third reason for believing the Bible to be the Word of God is the unity of the Book. This is an old argument, but a good one. The Bible is composed, as you probably know, of sixty-six parts, or books. It is oftentimes said that the Bible is not a book, but a library. This is partly true, partly false. It is true the Bible is a library, but at the same time it is the most intensely unified book of any book on earth.

The sixty-six books that compose the Bible were written by at least forty different authors. They were written in three different languages: Hebrew, Aramaic, and Greek. The period of their composition extends over at least fifteen hundred years. They were written in countries hundreds of miles apart. They were written by men on every plane of political and social life, from the king on the throne down to the herdsman and shepherd and fisherman and politician. They display every form of literary structure. In the Bible we find all kinds of poetry: epic poetry, lyric poetry, didactic poetry, elegy, and rhapsody. We find all kinds of prose as well: historic prose, didactic prose, theological treatise, epistle, proverb, parable, allegory, and oration.

In a book so composite, made up of such divergent parts, composed at such remote periods of time and under such diverse circumstances, what would we naturally expect? Variance and discord, utter lack of unity. What do we find? The most marvelous unity. Every part of the Bible fits every other part of the Bible; one ever-increasing, ever-growing thought pervades the whole.

The character of this unity is most significant. It is not a superficial unity, but a profound unity. On the surface, we often find apparent discrepancy and disagreement; but as we study, the apparent discrepancy and disagreement disappear, and the deep underlying unity appears. The more deeply we study, the more complete we find the unity to be.

The unity is also an organic one; that is, it is not the unity of a dead thing, like a stone, but of a living thing, like a plant. In the early books of the Bible, we have the germinating thought. As we go on, we have the plant, and further on the bud, and then the blossom, and then the ripened fruit. In Revelation we find the ripened fruit of Genesis.

How are we to account for it? This is another fact that demands accounting for, and as a practical person you have to deal with facts, not theories. You have to deal with realities, not mere speculations of secluded theologians, dreaming apart from the substantial realities of life. There is one easy and simple way to account for it, and only one rational way to account for it at all, namely, that behind the forty or more human authors was the one all-governing, all-controlling, all-superintending, all-shaping mind of God.

Suppose it is proposed to build in our capital city, Washington D.C., a temple that would represent the stone products of every state in America. The stones are to come from every state; some from the marble quarries of Marlboro, New Hampshire; others from the granite quarries of Quincy, Massachusetts; some from the brownstone quarries of Middletown, Connecticut; some from the white marble quarries at Rutland, Vermont; some from the gray sandstone quarries at Berea, Ohio; some from the porphyry quarries below Knoxville, Tennessee; some from the brownstone quarries at Kasota, Minnesota; some from the gypsum quarries of the far West; some stones from every state in America. The stones are to be of all conceivable sizes and shapes: some large, some small, some medium, some cubical, some spherical, some cylindrical, some conical, some trapezoidal, and some rectangular. Each stone is to be hewn into its final shape at the quarry from which it is taken. Not a stone is to be touched by mallet or chisel after it reaches its destination.

Finally, the stones arrive at Washington, and the builders go to work. As they build, they find that every stone fits into every other stone and into its place. They find that there is not one stone too many, or one stone too few.

At last the builders' work is done, and there stands before them a temple with its side walls, its buttresses, its naves, its arches, its choirs, its roof, its pinnacles, and its dome, perfect in every outline and in every detail. There is not one stone too many and not one stone too few, not one stone left over, and no niche or corner where one stone is lacking.

Yet, every stone was hewn into its final shape in the quarry from which it was taken. How would you account for it? There is one very simple way to account for it, and only one way to account for it at all, namely, that behind the individual quarrymen was the master architect who planned the whole building from the beginning and gave to each individual quarryman his specifications for the work.

Now, this is precisely what we find in that temple of eternal truth that we call the Bible. The stones for this masterpiece were quarried in places hundreds of miles apart and hundreds of years apart. They are stones of all conceivable sizes and shapes, and yet every stone fits into its place and fits with every other stone. The Book stands before you, a matchless temple of God's truth, perfect in every outline and every detail, not one stone too many and not one stone too few. Yet, every stone was cut into its final shape in the quarry from which it was taken. How are you to account for it? There is but one rational way to account for it, namely, that behind the human hands was the all-knowing mind of God that gave to each individual workman his specifications for the work. You cannot be honest and fair and get around it.

3

The Superiority of the Bible

So far I have given you three reasons why I believe the Bible to be the Word of God. The first reason was the testimony of Jesus Christ to that effect. We saw that Jesus Christ put the stamp of His authority on the entire Old Testament and the entire New Testament, and that if we accept the authority of Jesus Christ, we have to accept the entire Bible as being of divine origin and authority. Then we saw that we must accept the authority of Jesus Christ, for He was commended to us by five unmistakably divine testimonies.

My second reason was the fulfilled prophecies of the Bible. We saw that the Bible had the power of looking into the future and predicting with minuteness and exactness things that were to occur hundreds of years later. We saw that these prophecies were fulfilled to the letter. We determined that a Book that had this power of looking into the future and telling with minuteness, exactness, and precision things that were to come, must have for its author the only One in the universe who knows the end from the beginning—that is, God.

My third reason for believing the Bible to be the Word of God was the unity of the Book. We saw that the Bible is composed of sixty-six books. It was written by at least forty human authors over a period of at least fifteen hundred years. It displays every form of literary structure. Nevertheless, there is one all-pervading thought and purpose throughout the entire Book; every part of the Book fits together with every other part, and the Bible is the most thoroughly unified book of any book on earth. We saw that the only way to account for this undeniable and remarkable phenomenon is that behind the many human authors is the one all-governing, all-controlling, all-superintending, all-shaping mind of God.

THE BIBLE'S SUPERIOR TEACHINGS

My fourth reason for believing the Bible to be the Word of God is the immeasurable superiority of its teachings to those of all other books. It was the trend when I was studying in theological schools, to compare the teachings of the Bible with those of ethnic seers and philosophers, such as Socrates, Plato, Marcus Aurelius Antoninus, Epictetus, Isocrates, Seneca, Buddha, Zoroaster, Confucius, Mencius, and Mohammed. This is getting to be the trend again. Anyone who institutes such a comparison and puts the Bible in the same class with these other teachers, must be ignorant of the teachings of the Bible, or ignorant of the teachings of these ethnic seers and philosophers, or, what is more frequently the case, ignorant of both. There are three points of radical difference between the teachings of the Bible and those of any other book.

Nothing but the Truth

First, these other teachings contain truth, but truth mixed with error. The Bible contains nothing but truth. (See John 17:17.) There are gems of thought from these ethnic writers, but they are, as Joseph Cook called them years ago, "jewels picked out of the mud." For example, we are often asked, "Didn't Socrates teach most beautifully how a philosopher ought to die?" He did, but they forget to tell us that he also taught a woman of the town how to conduct her business that was not quite so nice. Again, they ask us, "Didn't Marcus Aurelius Antoninus teach most excellently about clemency?" He did. It is well worth reading. But they forget to tell us that he also taught that it was right to put people to death for no other crime than that of being Christians; and being himself emperor of Rome and having power to do it, he practiced what he preached.

"Didn't Seneca," they ask, "discourse finely about the advantages of poverty?" He did, but they forget to tell us that Seneca himself was at the time one of the worst spenders in Rome, his mansion's onyx tables alone costing a fabulous fortune. Moreover, he was the tutor under whose influence Nero, the most infamous emperor that Rome ever had, was brought up.

"Didn't Confucius," they ask again, "set forth admirably the duty of children to parents?" He did, but they forget to tell us that Confucius also taught that it was right to tell lies on occasion, and unblushingly said that he himself practiced lying on occasions. And there is perhaps nothing in which his most devoted followers, the Chinese, have followed so closely in the footsteps of their great master as in this matter of lying. The Chinese have reduced lying to a fine art, and some will tell anything to save face.

All of the Truth

The second point of difference is that these other writings contain part of the truth, while the Bible contains all of the truth. There is not a single known truth on moral or spiritual subjects that cannot be found within the covers of the Bible. This is a most remarkable fact: the Bible is an old book, yet man in all his thinking before and since the Bible was written has not discovered one single truth on moral or spiritual subjects that cannot be found within the covers of the Bible.

In other words, if all other books were destroyed and the Bible left, we would suffer no essential loss on moral and spiritual subjects; but if the Bible were destroyed and all other books left, the loss would be irreparable. Why is this if the Bible is merely a book by men like these other books?

Oftentimes I have challenged the people in my audience to bring forward one single truth on moral or spiritual subjects that I could not find within the Bible. It is quite conceivable that someone should succeed in doing this, for I do not pretend to know everything that is in the Bible—I have only been studying it a little over a quarter of a century—but no one has been able to do it yet.

More Truth Than All Other Books Combined

The third point of radical difference is this: the Bible contains more truth than all other books put together. You can go to all literature, ancient and modern—the literature of ancient Greece, ancient Rome, ancient India, ancient Persia, and ancient China, and all modern literature as well—glean from it all that is good, throw away all that is bad or worthless, bring together the result of your labor into one book, and even then you will not have a book that will take the place of the Bible. Why is it, if the Bible is merely a book by men like other books, that in all the thousands of years of men's thinking, in all the millions of books that they have produced, men have not been able, all of them put together, to produce as much real and priceless wisdom as is contained in this one Book? The answer is plain: other books are men's books; the Bible stands alone as God's Book.

The Bible's Strength against Every Attack

My fifth reason for believing the Bible to be the Word of God is its history; it has been omnipotent against all attacks. What man has made, man can destroy. But many centuries of most strenuous and determined assault have not been able to destroy or undermine intelligent faith in the Bible. Scarcely was the Bible given to the world before men discovered three things about it: first, that it condemned sin; second, that it demanded renunciation of self; and third, that it laid human pride in the dust. Men were not willing to give up sin, not willing to renounce self, not willing to have their pride laid in the dust; therefore, they hated the Book that made these demands.

Man's hatred of the Bible has been most intense and most active. Man after man has been determined to destroy this Book. Celsus tried it, with the brilliancy of his genius, and he failed. Then Porphyry tried it, with the depth of his philosophy, and he failed. Lucien tried it, with the keenness of his satire, and he failed. Then Diocletian came on the scene of action and tried other weapons; he used against the Bible all the military and political power of the strongest empire the world ever knew, at the height of its glory. He issued edicts that every Bible must be burned, but that failed. Stronger edicts were issued—that those who owned Bibles must be put to death—and that failed.

For many centuries the attack on the Bible has gone on. Every engine of destruction that human wisdom, human science, human philosophy, human wit, human satire, human force, and human brutality could use against a book have been used against this Book, and the Bible still stands. At times all the great men of earth have been against it, and only an obscure remnant for it, but still the Bible has more than held its own. It has today a firmer hold on the confidence and affection of the best and wisest men and women than it ever had before in the world's history. If the Bible had been man's book, it would have gone down and been forgotten centuries ago; but because there is in this Book not only the hiding of God's wisdom, but the hiding of His power, it has wonderfully fulfilled the words of Jesus: "Heaven and earth shall pass away, but my words shall not pass away" (Matt. 24:35).

At times it has seemed to some, amid the deafening roar of the enemies' artillery and the dense smoke of battle, that the Bible must have been defeated. But when the smoke has rolled up from the field of conflict, this impregnable citadel of God's eternal truth has stood unscathed, without one stone dislodged from foundation to highest parapet. Each new assault on the Bible has simply served to illustrate anew the absolute omnipotence of this God-given Book. In a way, I rejoice in every new attack that is made on the Bible. I tremble for certain weak-minded men and women who are willing to swallow anything that is said to be the consensus of the latest scholarship, but for the Bible itself I have no fears. A Book that has successfully withstood centuries of the assaults of the Devil's heaviest artillery is not going down before the air guns of modern criticism.

THE POWER OF THE BIBLE

My sixth reason for believing the Bible to be the Word of God is the influence of the Book, its power to lift men up to God. Every honest man must see and admit that there is a power in this Book to brighten, gladden, beautify, and ennoble human lives, to lift men up to God. This is a power no other book possesses. A stream can rise no higher than its source, and a Book that has an unparalleled power to lift men up to God must have come down from God in a way no other book has. In literally millions of cases, this Book has demonstrated its power to reach down to men and women in the deepest depths of iniquity and degradation and lift them up high, until they were fit for a place beside Christ upon the throne (Eph. 2:6).

I recall a man with a brilliant mind, but he was stupefied and brutalized and demonized by alcohol, and this man was an agnostic. I urged him to accept the Bible and the Christ of the Bible, but with a hollow laugh he said, "I don't believe in your Bible or your Christ. I am an agnostic." But, at last, sunken to the lowest depths of ruin, he threw his agnosticism to the wind and accepted this Book and the Christ of this Book. By the power of this Book, he was transformed into one of the truest, noblest, humblest men I know. What other book could do this?

This Book has power to lift not only individuals, but also nations, toward God. We owe all that is best in our modern civilization, in our political, commercial, and domestic life, to the influence of this Book. The man who attacks the Book is attacking the very foundations of all that is best in modern civilization. The man who attacks the Bible is the worst enemy that an individual or society has.

THE GOOD CHARACTER OF BIBLE BELIEVERS

Seventh, I believe the Bible to be the Word of God because of the character of those who accept it as such, and because of the character of those who reject it. These two things speak for the divine origin of this Book. Oftentimes, when a person says to me, "I firmly believe the Bible to be the Word of God," I see the purity, the beauty, the humility, the devotion to God and man that there is in his character. How near he lives to God! I feel like saying, "I am glad that you do believe the Bible to be the Word of God. The fact that one who lives so near to God and knows God as well as you do, believes the Bible to be His Book, is a confirmation of my own faith that it is."

On the other hand, oftentimes when a man with a self-confident toss of the head says, "I do not believe the Bible is the Word of God," I see the sinfulness or selfishness or smallness or sordidness of his life. How far he lives from God! I feel like saying, "I am glad that you do not believe the Bible. The fact that a man like you—who lives so far from God and knows God so little—doubts that the Bible is the Word of God, is a confirmation of my own faith that it is."

Do not misunderstand me. I do not mean by this that every man who professes to believe in the Bible is better than every man who rejects the Bible. What I do mean is this: show me a man who is living a life of absolute surrender to God, living under the control of the Spirit of God, living a life of devotion to the highest welfare of his fellowmen, living a life of humility and of prayer, and I will show you every time a man who believes the Bible to be God's Word. On the other hand, show me a man who denies or persistently questions whether the Bible is the Word of God, and I will show you a man who is leading either (mind you, I say "either," not "all") a life of greed for gold, or of lust, or of self-will, or of spiritual pride. I challenge any man to find me an exception. I have been looking for one around the world, and I have never found one. An attempt to find an exception has been made a number of times, but it is simply laughable to think of the suggested men as leading lives of humility and prayer, or to think of them as not leading lives of self-will. Anyone who has not surrendered absolutely to God is leading a life of self-will.

In other words, all who live nearest to God and know God best are sure that the Bible is God's Word. Those who have many doubts about it are those who are living farthest from God and know God least. Which will you believe?

Suppose that there is discovered in the city of Boston a manuscript that is said to be by Oliver Wendell Holmes, but there is great discussion among the critics as to whether or not

Oliver Wendell Holmes is the real author. Finally, it is submitted to a committee of critics for decision. It is discovered that all those critics who knew Oliver Wendell Holmes best, who lived in most intimate fellowship with him, who were most in harmony with his thought, are absolutely unanimous in their declaration that the manuscript is by him. Furthermore, those who question it are those who knew Oliver Wendell Holmes the least, who had the least fellowship with him, and who were least in harmony with his thought. Which would you believe?

That is a very simple question in literary criticism, much simpler than that which our modern critics so confidently undertook to solve, namely, who may be the seven different authors of a single verse in the Bible. This question they attempted to answer in that monumental joke book of the nineteenth century, the Polychrome Bible.[1]

Now, this is the precise case with the Bible. All who live nearest to God and know God best, all who are in most intimate fellowship with Him, are of absolutely one accord in say-

---

[1] In the Polychrome Bible, different colors were designated to different passages to indicate who wrote what. In some places, a single verse contained several colors, indicating several authors!

ing that the Bible is His work. Those who have the most doubts about it are those who live farthest from God and know Him least.

There is another significant fact, that the nearer men get to God, the more confident they become that the Bible is His Word. The farther they drift from God, the more doubt enters their hearts. This is a case that constantly occurs: a man who is a sinner and an unbeliever, by simply giving up his sin without further argument, is delivered from his unbelief. Can anyone cite one single instance of the opposite kind, where one was a sinner and a believer, and by giving up his sin lost his faith?

Furthermore, how often this occurs: a man who once lived a life of consecration and nearness to God, and enjoyed a serene and undisturbed faith that the Bible is God's Word, begins to prosper in the things of this world; and the love of money enters his heart, and he drifts away. He drifts from the out-and-out separation of his life to God, and as he drifts from God, he drifts into doubt and into lax views about the Bible. We see this today upon every hand—men who are becoming lax in their morals also becoming lax in their doctrine. Good morals and good theology go hand in hand; they are twin brothers. So true is this that oftentimes when men tell me that they are starting to doubt, I ask them the question, "What have you been doing?"

Once, walking in a university town, I saw on the street a little way ahead of me a young man whom I knew. I caught up with him and said to him, "Charlie, how are you getting along?" and with a self-satisfied look he said, "Well, to tell you the truth, Mr. Torrey, I am getting somewhat skeptical." I said, "Charlie, what have you been doing?" The poor boy blushed and dropped his head. Charlie had been sinning, and sin had given birth to doubt. This is how doubt has crept into the hearts of thousands of men today.

Where is the stronghold of the Bible? The pure, happy, unselfish home. Where is the stronghold of unbelief? The tavern, the gambling hell, the houses of prostitution. Suppose that I should come, a stranger to your city, and should go into one of your taverns with a Bible under my arm, lay my Bible down on the bar, order a glass of whisky straight, and add, "Make it big." What would happen? There would be great surprise. Quite likely the bartender would say, "Pardon me, but what is that book? Isn't that the Bible?" "Yes." "And what did you ask for—a tumbler of whisky straight?" "Yes, and make it big." He would not know what to make of it.

But, suppose I should enter the tavern and lay on the bar a copy of any work of Ingersoll or of Bradlaugh, a copy of the *Clarion,* or the *Agnostic Journal,* or *Freethinker,* or the most respectable infidel book or paper that there is, and order a glass of whisky straight. I would get it without a question or a look of surprise. It would be just what they would expect. The Bible and whisky do not go together. Unbelief and whisky do go together.

When I was in Belfast I made this remark, and at the close of the lecture a physician came to me laughing and said, "Yesterday we had an illustration of just what you said. After your afternoon Bible reading, my mother went into a licensed grocer's to get a little brandy for a friend who was ill. She had her Bible in her hand and, without thinking, was trying to put it into the bag that she carried. The clerk who was waiting on her said, "That's right, ma'am, hide it. The two don't go well together."

4

The Inexhaustible Book

In the three previous chapters I have given you seven reasons why I believe the Bible to be the Word of God. The first reason was the testimony of Jesus Christ to that effect. We saw that Jesus Christ put the stamp of His authority on the entire Old Testament and the entire New Testament, and that if we accept the authority of Jesus Christ, we are obliged to accept the entire Bible. We next saw that we must accept the authority of Jesus Christ, for He was commended to us by five unmistakably definite testimonies: first, by the testimony of the divine life that He lived; second, by the testimony of the divine words that He spoke; third, by the testimony of the divine works that He did; fourth, by the testimony of His divine influence on all subsequent history; and fifth, by the testimony of His resurrection from the dead, which was God's divine confirmation of the claims of Jesus Christ.

The second reason I gave was the Bible's fulfilled prophecies. We saw that the Bible had the power of looking into the future and predicting with minuteness, accuracy, and precision things that were to occur hundreds of years ahead, and that these prophecies had been fulfilled to the letter. We concluded that a book that had this power of looking into the future and telling with minuteness, accuracy, and precision things that were to come to pass centuries afterwards, must have for its author the only one in the universe who knows the end from the beginning—that is, God.

The third reason I gave for believing the Bible to be the Word of God was the unity of the Book. We saw that the Bible is composed of sixty-six books. It was written by at least forty human authors over a period of at least fifteen hundred years. It displays every form of literary structure. Nevertheless, there is one all-pervading thought and purpose throughout the entire Book; every part of the Book fits together with every other part; and the Bible is the most thoroughly unified book of any book on earth. We saw that the only way to account for this undeniable and remarkable phenomenon is that behind the many human authors is the all-governing, all-controlling, all-superintending, all-shaping mind of God.

The fourth reason for believing the Bible to be the Word of God was the immeasurable superiority of its teachings to those of all other books. We saw that there are three points of radical difference between the Bible and all other books: first, other books contain truth mixed with error, but the Bible contains nothing but truth; second, other books contain part of the truth, but the Bible contains all of the truth; and third, the Bible contains more truth than all other books combined.

The fifth reason was the history of the Book, its omnipotence against all attacks. We saw that what man had produced man could destroy, but that centuries of assault on the Bible had utterly failed to destroy the Book or to undermine confidence in it. Our sixth reason for believing the Bible to be the Word of God was its power to lift men up to God. We saw that the Bible has a power to lift men up to God that no other book possesses; therefore, it must have come down from God in a way no other book has.

Our seventh reason for believing the Bible to be the Word of God was the character of those who accept it as such and those who reject it. We saw that all the men and women who live nearest to God, and know God best, believe the Bible to be His Word, and that those who have the most doubts about it are those who live farthest from God and know God least.

THE INEXHAUSTIBLE DEPTH OF THE BIBLE

My eighth reason for believing the Bible to be the Word of God is the inexhaustible depth of the Book. What man has produced, man can exhaust. But centuries of study, by tens of thousands of the ablest minds, have been unable to exhaust the Bible. Many men of strongest intellect, of marvelous powers of penetration, of broadest culture, have given a lifetime to the study of the Bible, and no man who has really studied it has ever dreamed of saying that he has gotten to the bottom of the Book. Indeed, the deeper one digs into the Book, the more clearly he sees that there are still unfathomable depths of wisdom beneath him in this inexhaustible mine of truth.

Not only is this true of individuals; it is also true of generations of men. Thousands of men in cooperation with one another have delved into this mine, but they have never come close to exhausting it. There are still new treasures of truth awaiting each new student of the Word. New light is constantly breaking forth from the Word of God.

The human mind has been progressing through the centuries; we have outgrown every other book that belongs to the past. But far from outgrowing the Bible, we have not yet grown up to it. The Bible is not only up-to-date, but always ahead of date. The best interpretation of the most recent events of our own day is found in this old Book. If this Book were man's book, we would have fathomed it centuries ago, but the fact that it has proved itself unfathomable for many centuries is positive proof that in it are hidden the infinite treasures of the wisdom and knowledge of God.

A brilliant Unitarian writer has uttered one of the keenest sentences that was ever spoken or written by someone who denies the Bible's inspiration. (A Unitarian, to further define the term, also denies the doctrine of the Trinity and the deity of Jesus.) He said, "How irreligious to accuse an infinite God of putting His whole wisdom in so small a book!" I submit that that is keen, but this writer did not see how the keen edge of his Damascus blade could be turned against himself. What a testimony to the divine origin of this Book that such infinite wisdom could be packed into so small a space! The Bible is not such a very large book (I have a copy that I carry in my vest pocket), yet in a book that can be printed in so small a space, there are packed away such treasures of wisdom, that centuries of study by the world's best minds have been unable to exhaust it. How are we to account for this unquestionable fact? There is no one but God who could pack such infinite treasures of truth into so small a space.

NEARER TO GOD, NEARER TO THE BIBLE

My ninth reason for believing the Bible to be the Word of God is the fact that as I grow in knowledge and in character, in wisdom and in holiness, I grow toward the Bible. The nearer I get to God, the nearer I get to the Bible. When I began to really study the Bible, I had the same experience that every thoughtful student has had in the beginning of his studies. I found some things in the Bible that were difficult to understand, others that seemed unbelievable. I found that the teachings of one part of the Book seemed to flatly contradict the teachings of other parts of the Book. It seemed clear to me that if a certain teaching of the Bible were true, a certain other could not be. Like so many others, I accepted as much of the Bible as was wise enough to agree with me.

But as I went on studying the Bible, and as I went on growing in likeness to God, I found that my difficulties were disappearing—at first, one by one, then by twos, and then by scores, ever disappearing more and more. I found constantly that the nearer I got to God, the nearer I got to the Bible. Nearer still to God meant nearer still to the Bible. What is the inevitable mathematical conclusion? Two lines always converging as they draw near to a given point must meet when they reach that point. The nearer I got to God, the nearer I got to the Bible. When God and I meet, the Bible and I will meet. That is, the Bible was written from God's standpoint. There is no honest escaping of this conclusion.

Suppose I am to pass through a vast, dark, and dangerous forest for the first time. Before starting on this perilous tour, a guide is brought to me who has often been through the forest before, has conducted many a party through in safety, and has never led a single party astray. Under his leadership I begin my journey through the forest. We get along very nicely together for a ways, but after a time we come to a place where two roads diverge. The guide says to me, "The path to the right is the correct one to take."

However, the circumstances observed by my senses and analyzed by my reason clearly indicate that the road to the left is the road to take. I say to the guide, "I know that you have been through this forest time and time again. I know that you have conducted many a party through in safety. I have great confidence in your judgment on that account. But, in the present instance I believe you are wrong. The circumstances observed by my senses and analyzed by my reason clearly indicate that the road to the left is the road to take. Now, I have never been through this forest before, and you have; and I know that my reason and judgment are not infallible, but they are the best guide that I have, and I cannot throw them overboard. I must follow them." So I take the road to the left. I go about a mile and then come to an impassable swamp and have to go back and take the way the guide said.

We get along well together again for a ways, but again we come to a place where two paths diverge. This time the guide says, "The road to the left is the road to take." But, the circumstances observed by my senses and analyzed by my reason clearly indicate that the road to the right is the road to take, and again we have our little discussion. Again I say to the guide, "I know that you have passed through this forest time and time again. I know that you have never led a party astray. I have great confidence in your judgment on that account. But, the circumstances observed by my senses and analyzed by my reason tell me that the road to the right is the road to take. Now, I know that my reason and common sense are not infallible, but they are the best guide that I have, and I cannot throw them overboard." So, again, I go the way suggested by the circumstances observed by my senses and analyzed by my reason. I go about half a mile and then come to an impassable barrier of rock and have to go back and go the way the guide said.

Suppose that this should happen fifty times, and every time the guide proves right and my analyzing of the circumstances proves wrong. Do you not think that about the fifty-first time I would have reason and common sense enough to throw my ever-erring judgment to the wind and go the way the guide says?

This has been my exact experience with the Bible. Time and time again I came to the parting of the ways, where the Bible said one thing and my reason and common sense said another. Fool that I was, I threw the Bible overboard and went the way that my reason and common sense said. Every time I have had to come back and go the way the Bible said. I trust that the next time the Bible and I differ, I will have enough common sense to throw my ever-erring reason and judgment overboard and go the way the Bible says.

The most irrational thing in the world is what we call rationalism. Rationalism is an attempt to subject the teachings of infinite wisdom to the criticism of our finite judgment. Could anything possibly be more irrational than that? It never seems to occur to the rationalist that God can have a good reason for saying or doing a thing even if he, the rationalist, cannot see the reason. One of the greatest discoveries that I ever made was when it dawned on me that God might possibly know more than I know, and that God might possibly be right when to me He appears to be wrong.

THE TESTIMONY OF THE HOLY SPIRIT

My tenth reason for believing the Bible to be the Word of God is the testimony of the Holy Spirit to that fact. To the one who puts himself in the right attitude toward God and truth, the Holy Spirit bears direct testimony that the voice that speaks to him from the Bible is the voice of God.

Perhaps you often meet a godly old woman, not of very wide reading or culture, who still has a firm faith that the Bible is the Word of God. If you ask her why she believes the Bible to be the Word of God, she replies, "I *know* the Bible to be the Word of God." But, if you ask again, "*Why* do you believe it to be the Word of God?" she replies, "I *know* it to be the Word of God." And if still again you ask, "*Why* do you believe it to be the Word of God?" again she replies, "I *know* it to be the Word of God."

Very likely you give up and say, "Well, I will not disturb the old lady's faith" (no fear, you couldn't if you tried), "but she is beneath argument." You are mistaken; she is above argument. Jesus Christ says, "He that is of God heareth God's words" (John 8:47). Again Jesus Christ says, "My sheep hear my voice" (John 10:27). She is one of God's children and knows her Father's voice. She knows that the voice that speaks to her from the Bible is the voice of God. She is one of Christ's sheep, and she knows that the voice that speaks to her from the Bible is the voice of the true Shepherd.

I can tell you how you can come to that same position, where you will be able to distinguish God's voice and know that the voice that speaks to you from the Bible is the voice of God. Jesus Christ Himself tells us this in John

7:17 (RV), "If any man willeth to do his [God's] will, he shall know of the teaching, whether it be of God, or whether I speak from myself." The surrender of the will to God opens the eyes of the soul to see the truth of God. Jesus Christ does not demand that a man believe without evidence, but He does demand that a man put himself in that moral attitude toward God and the truth that makes him competent to appreciate evidence. There is nothing that so clarifies the human mind as the surrender of the will to God.

Some years ago I was lecturing to my students in Chicago on how to deal with skeptics and infidels. My lecture room in Chicago is open to all kinds and conditions of men, and oftentimes it is a motley crowd that gathers together—Christians and Jews, Roman Catholics and Protestants, believers, skeptics, infidels, agnostics, and atheists. At the close of this lecture, the wife of the late Dr. A. J. Gordon of Boston came to me and said, "Did you see the man sitting near me as you spoke?" I had noticed the man, because I had had a little conversation with him before. "Well," she added, "while you were speaking, I heard him say, 'I wish he would try it on me.'"

"I would be glad to."

"Well, there he is over in the corner."

I did not need to go to him, for when the others had gone out, he came to me and said, "Mr. Torrey, I do not wish to say anything discourteous, but really my experience contradicts everything that you have said to these students this morning."

I replied, "Have you done what I told these students to get the infidel or skeptic to do? Have you done what I guaranteed would bring the skeptic out of his unbelief into a clear belief that the Bible is God's Word and Jesus is God's Son?"

"Yes, I have done it all."

"Now," I said, "let's be definite about this." So I called my secretary and dictated something like this: "I believe that there is an absolute difference between right and wrong" (I did not say, "I believe that there is a God," for this man was an agnostic and neither affirmed nor denied the existence of God, and you have to begin where a man is), "and I hereby choose the right and will follow it wherever it carries me. I promise to make an honest search to find out if Jesus Christ is the Son of God, and if I find out that He is, I promise to accept Him as my Savior and confess Him publicly before the world." My secretary brought two copies of this, and I handed them to him and said, "Are you willing to sign this?"

He replied, "Certainly," and signed them both. He folded one and put it in his pocket. Then he added, "There is nothing in it. My case is very peculiar." His case was peculiar. He had been through Theosophy, Unitarianism, Spiritualism, and pretty much all other isms, and he was now an out-and-out agnostic.

"Another thing," I added. "Do you know that there is not a God?"

"No," he said, "I don't know that there is not a God. Any man is a fool to say he knows that there is not a God. I am an agnostic; I neither affirm nor deny."

I said, "Well, I know that there is a God, but that won't do you any good. Do you know that God does not answer prayer?"

"No, I do not know that God does not answer prayer. I do not believe that He answers prayer, but I do not *know* that He does not answer prayer."

"Well," I said, "I know that He does answer prayer, but that will not do you any good. But here is a possible clue to knowledge. You are a graduate of a British university?"

"Yes."

"Do you know the method of modern science? The method of modern science is this, that if one finds a possible clue to knowledge, he follows that possible clue to see what there may be in it. Here is a possible clue. Will you adopt the methods of modern science in religious investigation? Will you follow this possible clue to see what there may be in it? Will you offer this prayer, 'Oh, God, if there is any God, show me if Jesus Christ is Your Son or not; and if You show me that He is Your Son, I promise to accept Him as my Savior and confess Him as such before the world'?"

"Yes," he said, "I will do that, too, but there is nothing in it. My case is very peculiar."

"One more thing," I said. "John says in John 20:31, 'These are written, that ye might believe that Jesus is the Christ, the Son of God; and that believing ye might have life through his name.' Now, John tells us here that the gospel of John is written to show men the proof that Jesus is the Christ, the Son of God. Will you read the proof? Will you read the gospel of John?"

"I have read it again and again," he replied. "I can quote parts of it to you if you wish to hear them."

"No," I said, "but I want you to read it this time in a new way. Each time before you read offer this prayer: 'O God, if there is any God, show me what truth there is in the verses I am about to read. What you show me to be true, I promise to accept and take my stand upon.' Now, don't read too many verses at a time. Don't try to believe or disbelieve. Simply be open to conviction of the truth. Pay careful attention to what you read. When you have finished the gospel, report to me the result."

"Yes," he said, "I will do it all, but there is nothing in it. My case is very peculiar."

"Never mind," I said, and I went over again the three things he had promised to do, and we separated.

About two weeks later I was speaking on the South Side, and I saw this man in the hall. At the close of the meeting, he came to me and said, "There was something in that."

I replied, "I knew that before."

"Well," he said, "ever since I have done what I promised I would do, it is just as if I have been caught up and am being carried along by the Niagara River, and the first thing I know I will be a shouting Methodist."

I became a Methodist for the occasion and said, "Praise the Lord!"

I went East to lecture at some schools in Massachusetts. When I came back, there was a reception, and this man was present at the reception, and he came to me and said, "Are you busy?"

"Not too busy to speak to you," I replied.

We went into another room, and he said, "I cannot understand it. I cannot see how I ever listened to these men" (mentioning a number of infidel and Unitarian writers and speakers). "It is all nonsense to me now."

"Oh," I said, "the Bible explains that in 1 Corinthians 2:14: 'The natural man receiveth not the things of the Spirit of God: for they are foolishness unto him: neither can he know them, because they are spiritually discerned.' You have taken the right attitude towards truth, and God has opened your eyes to see the truth." He came into a clear faith in Jesus Christ as the Son of God and the Bible as the Word of God. If you doubt this story, try it for yourself, and you will have one of your own to tell.

The Bible is the Word of God. The voice that speaks to us from this Book is the voice of God. Some people say, "Suppose it is the Word; what of it?" Everything of it! If the Bible is the Word of God, then Jesus Christ is the Son of God, and there is no salvation for any of us outside of a living faith in Him. (See Acts 4:12.) This faith leads us to put all our trust for pardon in His atoning work on the cross of Calvary, and to surrender our wills and our lives absolutely to His control. Have you done this? Will you do it now?

5

Did Jesus Christ Really Rise from the Dead?

The resurrection of Jesus Christ is in many respects the most important fact in history. It is the Gibraltar of Christian evidences, the Waterloo of unbelief. If it can be proven to be a historic certainty that Jesus rose from the dead, then Christianity rests on an impregnable foundation. Every essential truth of Christianity is involved in the Resurrection. If the Resurrection stands, every essential doctrine of Christianity stands. If the Resurrection goes down, every essential doctrine of Christianity goes down. Intelligent skeptics and infidels realize this. A leading skeptic has recently said that there is no use wasting time discussing the other miracles; the essential question is, "Did Jesus Christ rise from the dead?" If He did, it is easy enough to believe the other miracles. If He did not, the other miracles must go. I am confident that this skeptic has correctly stated the case.

There are three separate arguments that prove the four gospels are true in what they say about the resurrection of Jesus Christ. The first argument is the external evidence for the authenticity and truthfulness of the gospel narratives. This is an altogether satisfactory argument, but I will not explain it in this book. The argument is long and intricate, and it would take many chapters to explain it satisfactorily. The other arguments are so completely sufficient that we can do without this, good as it is in its place.

In this chapter and the next, I will explain the second argument, which is the internal proofs of the Resurrection. In chapter seven I will explain the third argument, which is the circumstantial evidence of the Resurrection.

The second argument is based on the internal proofs of the truthfulness of the gospel records. This argument is thoroughly conclusive, and I will proceed to state it briefly. We will not assume anything whatsoever. We will not assume that the four gospel records are true history. We will not assume that the four gospels were written by the men whose names they bear. We will not even assume that they were written in the century in which Jesus is alleged to have lived, died, and risen again, nor in the next century, nor in the next. We will assume nothing whatsoever. We will start out with a fact that we all know to be true, namely, that we have the four gospels today, whoever wrote them. We will place the four gospels side by side and see if we can discern in them the marks of truth or of fiction.

FOUR SEPARATE ACCOUNTS

The first thing we notice as we compare these gospels with each other is that they are four separate and independent accounts. This appears plainly from the apparent discrepancies in the four different accounts. These apparent discrepancies are marked and many. If the four writers had gotten together and made up their stories, it would have been impossible to have so many and so marked discrepancies. It is therefore obvious that the four gospels were not written in collusion, that is, in secret agreement.

There is a harmony between the four accounts, but the harmony does not lie on the surface; it only comes out by protracted and thorough study. It is just the kind of harmony that would exist between accounts written by several different persons, each looking at the events from his own standpoint. It is just the kind of harmony that would not exist in four accounts manufactured in collusion. In four accounts manufactured in collusion, whatever harmony there was would have appeared on the surface; whatever discrepancy there was would only have come out by minute and careful study. In the Gospels, the apparent discrepancies lie on the surface. Whether true or false, these four accounts are separate and independent from one another. The four accounts supplement one another, one account sometimes reconciling apparent discrepancies between two others.

It is plain that these accounts must be either a record of facts that actually occurred, or else fiction. If fiction, they must have been fabricated in one of two ways, either independently of one another or in collusion with one another. They cannot have been made up independently; the agreements are too marked and too many. They cannot have been written in collusion; as already seen, the apparent discrepancies are too numerous and too noticeable. So, they were not made up independently and not made up in collusion. Therefore, it is evident that they were not made up at all. They are a true relation of facts as they actually occurred.

EYEWITNESS ACCOUNTS

The next thing that we notice is that these accounts bear striking indications of having been derived from eyewitnesses. The account of an eyewitness is readily distinguishable from that of one who is merely retelling what others have told him. Anyone who is accustomed to weighing evidence in court or in historical study soon learns how to distinguish the account of an eyewitness from mere hearsay evidence. Any careful student of the gospel records of the Resurrection will readily detect many marks of an eyewitness.

Some years ago, when I was lecturing at an American university, a gentleman was introduced to me as being a skeptic. I asked him what course of study he was pursuing. He replied that he was pursuing a postgraduate course in history with plans to be a history professor. I said, "Then you know that the account of an eyewitness differs in marked respects from the account of one who is simply telling what he has heard from others?"

He replied, "Yes."

I then asked, "Have you carefully read the four gospel accounts of the resurrection of Christ?"

He answered, "I have."

"Tell me, have you not noticed clear indications that they were derived from eyewitnesses?"

"Yes," he replied, "I have been greatly struck by this in reading the accounts." Anyone else who carefully and intelligently reads them will be struck by the same fact.

STRAIGHTFORWARD ACCOUNTS

The third thing that we notice about these gospel narratives is their naturalness, straightforwardness, artlessness, and simplicity. The accounts indeed have to do with the supernatural, but the accounts themselves are most natural. There is an absolute absence of all attempt at coloring and effect. The Gospels are the simple, straightforward telling of facts as they occurred.

It sometimes happens that when a witness is on the witness stand, the story he tells is so artless, so straightforward, so natural—there is such an entire absence of any attempt at coloring and effect—that his testimony alone bears weight, independent of his character or past. As we listen to his story, we say to ourselves, "This man is telling the truth." We become more convinced, and practically certain, when we hear several independent witnesses of this sort, all bearing testimony to the same essential facts but with different details. We become even more certain when one witness tells what another had omitted and a third unconsciously reconciles apparent discrepancies between the two.

This is the precise case with the four gospel narratives of the resurrection of Christ. The gospel authors do not seem to have reflected at all on the meaning or bearing of many of the facts that they relate. They simply tell exactly what they saw, in all simplicity and straightforwardness, leaving the philosophizing to others. Dr. William Furness, the great Unitarian scholar and critic, who certainly was not overly disposed to favor the supernatural, said, "Nothing can exceed in artlessness and simplicity the four accounts of the first appearance of Jesus after His crucifixion. If these qualities are not discernible here, we must despair of ever being able to discern them anywhere."

Suppose we find four accounts of the battle of Monmouth. Nothing decisive is known as to the authorship of these accounts, but when we lay them side by side, we find that they are clearly independent accounts. We find, furthermore, striking indications that they are from eyewitnesses. We find them all marked by that artlessness, simplicity, and straightforwardness that carry conviction. We find that, while apparently disagreeing in minor details, they agree substantially in their account of the battle. Even though we have no knowledge of the authorship or date of these accounts, will we not in the absence of any other account say, "Here are true accounts of the battle of Monmouth"?

Now, this is exactly the case with the four gospel narratives: they are clearly separate and independent from one another; they bear the clear marks of having been derived from eyewitnesses; they are characterized by an unrivaled artlessness, simplicity, and straightforwardness; they disagree on the surface about minor details but agree perfectly about the great essential facts related. If we are fair and honest, are we not logically driven to say, "Here is a true account of the resurrection of Jesus"?

UNINTENTIONAL EVIDENCE

The next thing that we notice is the unintentional evidence of words, phrases, and accidental details. It often happens that when a witness is on the stand, the unintentional evidence that he gives by words and phrases that he uses, and by accidental details that he introduces, is more convincing than his direct testimony. These accidental slips are not the testimony of the witness, but the testimony of the truth to itself. The gospel stories abound in evidence of this sort.

Take as a first instance the fact that, in all the gospel records of the Resurrection, we are told that Jesus was not at first recognized by His disciples when He appeared to them after His resurrection. (See Luke 24:16; John 20:14; 21:4.) We are not told why this is so, but if we think about it a while, we can soon discover why it is so. But the gospel narratives simply record the fact without attempting to explain it. If the stories were fictitious, they would never have been made up in this way. The writers would have seen at once the objection that would have arisen in the minds of those who did not wish to believe in the Resurrection, that is, that it was not really Jesus whom the disciples saw. Why then is the story told this way? For the very evident reason that the writers were not making the story up for effect, but were recording events precisely as they occurred. This was the way it occurred, and therefore this is the way in which they told it. It is not a fabrication of imaginary incidents, but an exact record of facts accurately observed and accurately recorded.

Take a second instance. In all the gospel records of the appearances of Jesus after His resurrection, there is not a single recorded appearance to an enemy or opponent of Christ. All the appearances were to those who were already believers. Why this was so, we can easily see by a little thought, but nowhere in the Gospels are we told why it was so. If the stories were made up, they certainly would never have been made up in this way. If the Gospels are, as some would have us believe, fabrications constructed one hundred, two hundred, or three hundred years after the alleged events recorded, when all the actors were dead and gone, Jesus would have been represented as appearing to Caiaphas and Annas, and Pilate and Herod, and confounding them by his reappearance from the dead. But there is no suggestion of anything of this kind in the gospel stories. Every appearance is to one who is already a believer. Why is this so? For the very evident reason that this was the way that things occurred, and the gospel narratives are not concerned with producing a story for effect, but with simply recording events precisely as they occurred and as they were observed.

We find still another instance in the fact that the recorded appearances of Jesus after His resurrection were only occasional. He would appear in the midst of His disciples, then disappear, and not be seen again perhaps for several days. Why this was so, we can easily discern. Jesus was weaning His disciples from their past communion with Him in the body to prepare them for the communion in the Spirit they would experience in days to come. We are not, however, told this in the gospel narrative; we are left to discover it for ourselves. It is doubtful that the disciples themselves at the time realized the meaning of the facts. If they had been making up a story to produce effect, they would have represented Jesus as being with them constantly, as living with them, eating and drinking with them day after day. Why then is the story told as recorded in the four gospels? Because this is the way that it had all occurred, and the gospel writers were simply concerned with giving an exact representation of the facts as witnessed by themselves and by others.

We find another very striking instance in the record of Jesus' words to Mary at their first meeting after His resurrection. Jesus is recorded as saying to Mary, "Touch me not; for I am not yet ascended to my Father" (John 20:17). We are not told why Jesus said this to Mary. We are left to discover the reason for ourselves, if we can. The commentators have had a great deal of trouble discovering it. They vary widely from one another in their explanations of the words of Jesus. Go to the commentaries, and you will find that one commentary gives one reason, another gives another reason, and another gives another reason. And I have a reason of my own that I have never seen in any commentary.

Why, then, is this little utterance of Jesus put in the gospel record without a word of explanation, since it has taken centuries to explain and is not altogether satisfactorily explained yet? Certainly a writer making up a story would not add a little detail without apparent meaning and without any attempt to explain it. Stories that are made up are made up for a purpose; details that are inserted are inserted for a purpose, a purpose that is more or less obvious. But centuries of study have not been able to find out the reason why this is inserted. Why, then, is it there? Because this is exactly what happened. This is what Jesus said; this is what Mary heard; this is what Mary told; and therefore this is what John recorded. We do not have fiction here, but an accurate record of words spoken by Jesus after His resurrection.

Another incidental detail in the gospel narrative that is decisive proof of its historical accuracy, is found in John 19:34. We are told that when one of the soldiers pierced the side of our crucified Lord with a spear, immediately there came out blood and water. The reason of this we are not told. In fact, the writer could not have known the reason. There was no man on earth at the time who had sufficient knowledge of physiology to know the reason. It was only centuries afterwards that the physiological reason was discovered. The distinguished medical authority, Dr. Simpson, of Edinburgh University, the discoverer of chloroform, wrote during his lifetime an excellent brochure in which he showed on scientific grounds that Jesus Christ died from what is called in scientific language "extravasation of the blood," or, in popular language, "a broken heart." When one dies in this way, the arms are thrown out (of course, Jesus' arms were already stretched out on the cross); there is a loud cry (such as Jesus uttered, "My God, my God, why hast thou forsaken me?" [Matt. 27:46]); the wall that separates the serum from the blood is ruptured; and the serum and the blood flow together. When the Roman spear was driven into the heart of Jesus, the serum (that is, the water) and the blood gushed out.

This is the scientific explanation of the recorded fact, but John did not know this explanation. No one then living knew it; no one knew it for centuries afterwards. Is it conceivable that a writer, in making up a story that never happened, inserted a fact that has a strict scientific explanation, an explanation that neither he nor anyone living at the time could possibly have known? Of course not. How, then, did it come to be recorded in this way? Because this is precisely what occurred. Though John did not know the explanation, he observed the fact, recorded the fact as observed, and let time and scientific discovery prove the accuracy of what he told. Beyond a doubt, we have no fiction here, but an exact record of what occurred. In the next chapter, I will give even more striking illustrations of the self-evident and undeniable truthfulness of the gospel accounts of the Resurrection.

6

The Gospel Stories of
the Resurrection

In the last chapter, we began to consider the question, "Did Jesus really rise from the dead?" We started out without assuming anything whatsoever. We did not assume that the four gospels are true. We did not assume that the four gospels were written by the men whose names they bear. We did not even assume that they were written in the same century in which they allegedly occurred, nor the next century, nor the next.

We started with the obvious fact that we have the four gospels. Regardless of whether they are true or false, and regardless of who may have written them, we certainly have them. We laid these four gospels side by side and tried to discover by studying them whether they are a record of events that actually occurred or whether they are fiction. The first thing that we discovered was that they are separate and independent accounts. If fiction, they must have been fabricated in one of two ways, either independently of one another, or else in collusion with one another. We saw that they could not have been fabricated in collusion; the apparent discrepancies were too numerous and too noticeable. We saw that they could not have been made up independently; the agreements were too marked and too many. Not made up in collusion, not made up independently, then not made up at all. That is, they contain a true relation of facts as they actually occurred.

We saw, in the next place, that each of the gospel accounts bore striking indications of having been derived from eyewitnesses. We noted their artlessness, straightforwardness, and simplicity. We saw that it often happens that when a witness is on the stand, the story he tells is so artless, straightforward, simple, and natural that it carries conviction regardless of any knowledge we may have of the witness or of his character. We saw that each one of the gospel stories had these characteristics, which were clear proof of the truthfulness of the stories recorded.

We noticed, in the next place, the unintentional evidence of words, phrases, and accidental details. We saw that often when an eyewitness is on the stand, that the unintentional evidence he gives by words, phrases, and accidental details is more effective than his direct testimony, because it is not the testimony of the witness, but the testimony of the truth to itself. We gave a number of illustrations of this; we will give even more in this chapter.

Take a look at John 20:24–25:

But Thomas, one of the twelve, called Didymus, was not with them when Jesus came. The other disciples therefore said unto him, We have seen the Lord. But he said unto them, Except I shall see in his hands the print of the nails, and put my finger into the print of the nails, and thrust my hand into his side, I will not believe.

How true to life all this is. It is in perfect harmony with what is said about Thomas elsewhere. Thomas was the chronic doubter in the apostolic group, the man who always looked on the dark side, the man who was governed by the testimony of his senses. When Jesus said in John 11:15 that He was going again into Judea, it was Thomas who despondently

said, "Let us also go, that we may die with
him" (John 11:16). When Jesus said in John
14:4, "Whither I go ye know, and the way ye
know," it was Thomas who replied, "Lord, we
know not whither thou goest; and how can we
know the way?" (John 14:5). And it is he who
now says, "Except I shall see in his hands the
print of the nails, and put my finger into the
print of the nails, and thrust my hand into his
side, I will not believe." Is this made up, or is it
life? To make it up would require a literary art
that far exceeded the ability of the author.

Read about John and Peter in John 20:4–6:

*So they ran both together: and the other
disciple did outrun Peter, and came first
to the sepulchre. And he stooping down,
and looking in, saw the linen clothes lying; yet went he not in. Then cometh Simon Peter following him, and went into
the sepulchre.*

This is again in striking keeping with
what we know of the men. Mary, returning
hurriedly from the tomb, bursts in on the two
disciples and cries, "They have taken away the
Lord out of the sepulchre, and we know not
where they have laid him" (John 20:2). John
and Peter spring to their feet and run at top
speed to the tomb.

John was the younger of the two disciples. We are not told this in the narrative, but we learn it from other sources. Being younger, he is faster than Peter and reaches the tomb first; but, having a reverent disposition, he does not enter the tomb, but simply stoops down and looks in. Impetuous, older Peter comes lumbering along behind as fast as he can, but as soon as he reaches the tomb, he never waits a moment outside, but plunges headlong in. Is this made up, or is it life? The writer was certainly a literary genius if these events did not occur just like this. There is also, incidentally, a touch of local accuracy in the report. When one visits today the tomb that scholars now accept as the real burial place of Christ, he will find himself unconsciously having to stoop down to look in.

Look now at John 21:7:

Therefore that disciple whom Jesus loved saith unto Peter, It is the Lord. Now when Simon Peter heard that it was the Lord, he girt his fisher's coat unto him, (for he was naked,) and did cast himself into the sea.

Here, again, we have the unmistakable marks of truth and life. Recall the circumstances. The apostles have gone at Jesus' commandment into Galilee to meet Him there. (See Matthew 26:32; 28:7.) Jesus does not appear at once. Simon Peter, with the fisherman's passion still strong in his bones, says, "I go a fishing," and the others say, "We also go with thee" (John 21:3). They fish all night and catch nothing. In the early dawn, Jesus stands on the shore, but the disciples do not recognize Him in the dim light. Jesus says to them, "Children, have ye any meat?" and they answer, "No" (John 21:5). He tells them to cast the net on the right side of the boat and they will find.

When the cast is made, they are not able to draw the net in because of the multitude of fishes. In an instant, John, the man of quick, spiritual perception, says, "It is the Lord" (John 21:7). No sooner does Peter, the man of impulsive action, hear this, than he grips his fisher's coat, throws it about his naked form, throws himself overboard, and strikes out for shore to reach his Lord.

Is this made up, or is it life? This is certainly not fiction. If some unknown author of the fourth gospel made this up, he is the master literary artist of the ages, and we should lower every other name in the literary hall of fame and place his above them all.

Take another illustration, John 20:15:

> *Jesus saith unto her, Woman, why weep-*
> *est thou? whom seekest thou? She, sup-*
> *posing him to be the gardener, saith*
> *unto him, Sir, if thou have borne him*
> *hence, tell me where thou hast laid him,*
> *and I will take him away.*

Surely, here is a literary touch that surpasses the art of any man of that day, or any day. Mary had gone into the city and notified Peter and John that she had found the sepulcher empty. They start to run to the sepulcher. Since Mary has already made the journey twice, they easily get there first, but wearily and slowly she makes her way back to the tomb. Peter and John are long gone when she reaches it. Brokenhearted, thinking that the tomb of her beloved Lord has been desecrated, she stands outside, weeping. There are two angels sitting in the tomb, one at the head and the other at the foot where the body of Jesus had lain, but the grief-stricken woman has no eye for angels. They say to her, "Woman, why weepest thou?" and she replies, "Because they have taken away my Lord, and I know not where they have laid him" (John 20:13).

Mary hears footsteps in the leaves behind her, and she turns around to see who is coming. She sees Jesus standing there, but, blinded by tears and despair, she does not recognize her Lord. Jesus says to her, "Why weepest thou? whom seekest thou?" (John 20:15). She supposes it is the gardener who is talking to her and says, "Sir, if thou have borne him hence, tell me where thou hast laid him, and I will take him away" (John 20:15). Now, remember who it is that makes this offer and what she offers to do: a weak woman offers to carry away a full-grown man. Of course she could not do it, but how true to a woman's love, which always forgets its weakness and never stops at impossibilities. There is something to be done, and she says, "I will do it." "Tell me where thou hast laid him, and I will take him away" (John 20:15). Is this made up? Never! This is life! This is reality! This is truth!

Take still another illustration, Mark 16:7:

But go your way, tell his disciples and Peter that he goeth before you into Galilee: there shall ye see him, as he said unto you.

"But go your way, tell his disciples and Peter." What I wish you to notice here are the two words, "and Peter." Why "and Peter"? Was not Peter one of the disciples? Surely he was; he was the very head of the apostolic group. Why then "and Peter"? No explanation is furnished in the text, but reflection shows that it was the utterance of love towards the despondent, despairing disciple, who had denied his Lord three times. If the message had simply been to the disciples, Peter would have said, "Yes, I was once a disciple, but I can no longer be counted as such. I denied my Lord three times on that awful night with oaths and curses. He doesn't mean me." But our tender, compassionate Lord, through His angelic messengers, sends the message, "Go, tell His disciples, and whoever you tell, be sure you tell poor, weak, faltering, brokenhearted Peter."

Is this made up, or is this a real picture of our Lord? I pity the man who is so dull that he can imagine that this is fiction. Incidentally, let it be noticed that this is recorded only in the gospel of Mark, which is well known as Peter's gospel. As Peter dictated to Mark what to record, with tearful eyes and grateful heart he likely turned to him and said, "Mark, be sure you put that in, 'Tell his disciples *and Peter*' (Mark 16:7, italics added)."

Look now at John 20:27–29:

Then saith he to Thomas, Reach hither thy finger, and behold my hands; and

*reach hither thy hand, and thrust it into
my side: and be not faithless, but believing. And Thomas answered and said
unto him, My Lord and my God. Jesus
saith unto him, Thomas, because thou
hast seen me, thou hast believed: blessed
are they that have not seen, and yet have
believed.*

Note here both the action of Thomas and
the rebuke of Jesus. Each is too characteristic
to be attributed to the art of some master of
fiction. Thomas had not been with the disciples
at the first appearance of our Lord. (See John
20:24.) But a week had passed by; another
Lord's Day had come. This time Thomas
makes sure of being present; if the Lord is to
appear, he will be there. If he had been like
some modern skeptics, he would have taken
pains to be away; but doubter though he was,
he was an honest doubter and wanted to know.

Suddenly, Jesus stands in the midst. He
says to Thomas, "Reach hither thy finger, and
behold my hands; and reach hither thy hand,
and thrust it into my side: and be not faithless,
but believing" (John 20:27). Thomas's eyes are
opened at last. His long dammed-up faith bursts
every barrier and, sweeping on, carries Thomas
to a higher height than any other disciple had

gone yet. Exultingly and adoringly he cries, as he looks up into the face of Jesus, "My Lord and my God" (John 20:28).

Then Jesus tenderly, but oh, how searchingly, rebukes him. "Thomas," He says, "because thou hast seen me, thou hast believed: blessed are they that have not seen, and yet have believed" (John 20:29). In other words, blessed are they who are so eager to find and so quick to see and so ready to accept the truth that they do not wait for visual demonstration, but are ready to accept truth on sufficient testimony. Is this made up, or is this life? A record of facts as they occurred, or a fictitious story by some master writer?

Now read John 21:21–22:

Peter seeing him saith to Jesus, Lord, and what shall this man do? Jesus saith unto him, If I will that he tarry till I come, what is that to thee? follow thou me.

Let me explain the setting of these words. The disciples are on the beach of Galilee. Breakfast is over, and Jesus has told Peter how he is to glorify Him by dying a martyr's death. Jesus then starts to walk down the beach, and He says to Peter, "Follow me" (John 21:19).

Peter starts out to follow, but looking back over his shoulder to see what the others are doing, he sees John also following. With characteristic curiosity he says, "Lord, if I am to die for You, 'what shall this man do?' (John 21:21)."

Jesus never answered questions of mere curiosity about others, but He pointed the questioner to his own duty. On another occasion, when one came to Him with the question, "Are there few that be saved?" (Luke 13:23), He answered the questioner by telling him to see to it that he is saved himself.

So, now He points curious Peter away from questions that do not concern him to his own immediate duty. He says, "If I will that he tarry till I come, what is that to thee? follow thou me" (John 21:22). Is this made up, or is this life and reality?

Turn to other verses in the same chapter, John 21:15–17:

> *So when they had dined, Jesus saith to Simon Peter, Simon, son of Jonas, lovest thou me more than these? He saith unto him, Yea, Lord; thou knowest that I love thee. He saith unto him, Feed my lambs. He saith to him again the second time, Simon, son of Jonas, lovest thou me? He saith unto him, Yea, Lord; thou knowest*

> *that I love thee. He saith unto him, Feed*
> *my sheep. He saith unto him the third*
> *time, Simon, son of Jonas, lovest thou*
> *me? Peter was grieved because he said*
> *unto him the third time, Lovest thou me?*
> *And he said unto him, Lord, thou know-*
> *est all things; thou knowest that I love*
> *thee. Jesus saith unto him, Feed my*
> *sheep.*

I want you to pay special attention to the words, "Peter was grieved because he said unto him the third time, Lovest thou me?" Why did Jesus ask Peter three times, "Lovest thou me?" And why was Peter grieved because Jesus asked him three times? We are not told in the text, but if we read it in the light of Peter's threefold denial of his Lord, we will understand it. Since Peter had denied his Lord three times, Jesus gave Peter three opportunities to reassert his love. But all this, tender as it was, brought back to Peter's mind that awful night when, in the courtyard of Annas and Caiaphas, he had denied his Lord three times. (See John 18:12–18; 25–27.) Therefore, "Peter was grieved because he said unto him the third time, Lovest thou me?" (John 21:17).

Is this made up? Did the writer make it up with the fact of Peter's denial in view? If he did, he surely would have mentioned it. No, this is not fiction; this is simply reporting what actually occurred.

The accurate truthfulness of the record comes out even more strikingly in the Greek than in the English version. Two different words are used for love. Jesus, in asking Peter "Lovest thou me?" (John 21:15, 16, 17), uses a strong word for love, a word for a higher form of love. Peter, in replying, "Lord; thou knowest that I love thee" (John 21:15, 16), uses a weaker but a more tender word meaning "fondness." Essentially, he is saying, "Lord, I am fond of You." Jesus uses the stronger word the second time: "Lovest thou me?"; and a second time Peter replies, using the weaker word. In His third question, Jesus comes down to Peter's level and uses the weaker word that Peter had used, and Peter replies, "Lord, thou knowest all things; thou knowest that I love thee" (John 21:17), using the same weaker word.

Notice, again, the appropriateness of the way in which Jesus reveals Himself to different people after His resurrection. To Mary, He reveals Himself simply by calling her by name. Read John 20:16: "Jesus saith unto her, Mary. She turned herself, and saith unto him, Rabboni; which is to say, Master." What a delicate touch we have here. Mary, as we saw a few moments ago, is standing outside the tomb overcome with grief. She has not recognized her Lord, though He has spoken to her; she has mistaken Him for the gardener. She has said, "Sir, if thou have borne him hence, tell me where thou hast laid him, and I will take him away" (John 20:15). Then Jesus utters just one word; He says, "Mary" (John 20:16). As that name comes trembling on the morning air, uttered with the old familiar tone, spoken as no one else had ever spoken it, instantly her eyes are opened. She falls at His feet and tries to clasp them, and she looks up into His face and cries, "Rabboni; my Master."

Is that made up? No, this is life. This is Jesus, and this is a woman who loved Him. An unknown author of the second, third, or fourth century could never have produced such a masterpiece as this. Unquestionably, we stand here face to face with reality, with life, with Jesus and Mary as they actually were.

To the two men on the road to Emmaus, He made Himself known in the breaking of bread. Read Luke 24:30–31:

And it came to pass, as he sat at meat with them, he took bread, and blessed it, and brake, and gave to them. And their

*eyes were opened, and they knew him;
and he vanished out of their sight.*

They knew Him in the breaking of bread.
Why? The gospel writer ventures no explanation, but it is not hard to read between the
lines and find the explanation. In each one of
the Gospels, emphatic mention is made of Jesus' returning thanks at meals. (See Matthew
15:36; Mark 8:6; Luke 22:19; John 6:11.) There
was something very characteristic in the way
He returned thanks. It was very real and very
different from the way others returned thanks.
It was obvious that when Jesus prayed, He approached the very presence of God; His prayers
were utterly unlike the formal, unreal prayers
of others. Therefore, the moment Jesus lifted
up His eyes and gave thanks, the eyes of the
two men were opened, and they knew Him.
This, too, is reality and life, not fiction.

To Thomas, the man governed by his
senses, He made Himself known by exhibiting
the marks of the nails in His hands and the
hole in His side. To John and Peter, He made
Himself known as at the beginning (see Luke
5:4–10), in the miraculous catch of fish. Everywhere, in each minute detail, the narrative is
consistent and true to life. Could the Gospels
be fiction? Impossible!

Here is one more illustration. Read carefully John 20:7: "And the napkin, that was about his head, not lying with the linen clothes, but wrapped together in a place by itself." How strange that such a little detail as this should be added to the story, with absolutely no attempt at an explanation. But, how deeply significant this little unexplained detail is.

When I was studying at a theological seminary, an upperclassman came home one Sunday afternoon from his Bible class much disgusted. He taught a class of young working women, who were about twenty years of age. He said, "One of my scholars asked me a stupid question today. She asked me if there was any significance in the napkin being wrapped together in a place by itself. How stupid! How could there be any significance in that?" But, in reality, the problem was not a stupid working girl, but a stupid teacher. The napkin being by itself has the deepest significance. Let me explain.

Jesus Christ is dead. For three days and three nights, from Wednesday evening at sunset until Saturday evening at sunset, His body has lain cold and silent in the sepulcher, as truly dead as a body was ever dead. But, at last the appointed hour has come; the breath of God sweeps through the sleeping and silent body. In that supreme moment of His earthly life, that supreme moment of human history when Jesus rises triumphant over death and Satan, there is no flurry of activity on His part. He rises with that same majestic self-composure and serenity that marked His whole career.

He has the same divine calm that He displayed on the storm-tossed sea of Galilee when His frightened disciples shook Him from His slumber and said, "Master, carest thou not that we perish?" (Mark 4:38). Even then, He arose serenely on the deck of the tossing vessel and said to the raging waves and winds, "Be still" (Mark 4:39), and there was a great calm.

Likewise, now, in this sublime, this amazing moment of His resurrection, He does not excitedly tear the napkin from His face and throw it aside. Without any human haste or disorder whatsoever, He takes it calmly from His head, rolls it up, and lays it neatly by itself.

Was that made up? Never! We do not see in the Gospels a delicate masterpiece of a fiction writer. We read the simple narrative of a unique life that was actually lived here on the earth, a life so exquisitely beautiful that one cannot read it with an honest and open mind without feeling tears coming to his eyes.

However, I hear someone saying, "These are little things." True, but it is from that very fact that they gain much of their significance. It is in just such little things that fiction would give itself away. Fiction displays its difference from fact in the small things. In the great outstanding outlines, a writer can make fiction look like truth; but when it is examined closely by a careful reader, it is soon detected that it is not reality, but fabrication. However, the more closely we examine the gospel narratives, the more we become impressed with their truthfulness. The artlessness and naturalness and self-evident truthfulness of the narratives, down to the minutest detail, surpass all the possibilities of the writer's art.

In the next chapter, we will consider the circumstantial evidence for the resurrection of Christ.

7

The Circumstantial Evidence
of the Resurrection

In the last two chapters, we considered
some of the internal proofs of the truthfulness of the gospel story. We started out
without assuming anything. We did not assume that the four gospels are true. We did not
assume that they were written by Matthew,
Mark, Luke, and John. And we did not assume
that they were written in the first century, or
the second, or the third. We assumed nothing
whatsoever, but we simply laid the gospels side
by side to see what we could learn from them.

We discovered that the four gospels contain separate and independent accounts of the
resurrection of Christ. We saw that these gospel stories must be either a record of facts that
actually occurred, or else fiction. If fiction, they

must have been fabricated in one of two ways—either independently of one another, or in a cooperative effort. We saw that they could not have been fabricated independently of one another, because the agreements are too marked and too many. We saw that they could not have been fabricated cooperatively, because the apparent discrepancies are too numerous and too noticeable. Therefore, they were neither fabricated independently nor fabricated cooperatively. We were therefore driven to the conclusion that they were not fabricated at all, but they are a true record of facts that actually occurred.

We saw, in the next place, that each one of the four gospels bears the clear marks of having been derived from eyewitnesses. We then noted the artlessness, straightforwardness, and simplicity of the narratives, the entire absence of all attempt at coloring or effect. These are the certain marks of a true witness. We noted, in the next place, that often when a witness is on the stand, the unintentional evidence of words and phrases that he uses is more conclusive than his direct testimony, because it is not the testimony of the witness, but the testimony of the truth to itself. We then examined a large number of these unintentional testimonies in the Gospels, conclusively showing that the gospel stories could not have been made up. Beyond a doubt, they are the accurate representation of things that actually occurred.

In this chapter, we will examine the circumstantial evidence for the resurrection of Christ. By circumstantial evidence, we mean certain proven facts that demand for their explanation the fact that we are seeking to prove. For example, a man was once found murdered; the only clue leading to the murderer was the point of a knife blade that was found broken off in his heart. With this clue, the detectives went to work. A knife was found with a broken blade. The jagged edges of the broken blade matched exactly the notches in the point that had been found in the heart. Moreover, there were traces of blood on the point and the blade, and the traces of blood on the point matched the traces of blood on the blade. This circumstantial evidence was taken as proof that the murder was committed with that knife.

Here is another illustration. A bolt of cloth was stolen from a certain manufacturer; a search was made for the bolt of cloth. A bolt of cloth was found. The manufacturer claimed it was his stolen bolt, but the man who possessed the bolt claimed that it had come from a completely different factory. However, when the bolt of cloth was taken to the factory where the crime took place, the holes at each end of the bolt of cloth fit exactly on the tenterhooks of the factory. But, when it was taken to the factory from which the man claimed to have obtained it, the holes in the end of the bolt of cloth did not fit at all on the tenterhooks of that factory. This circumstantial evidence was considered proof that the bolt of cloth had come from the factory where it fit on the tenterhooks.

There is an abundance of this type of evidence in favor of the resurrection of Christ from the dead. There are certain proven facts that can only be accounted for by the resurrection of Christ.

Beyond a question, the foundational truth preached in the early years of the church was the Resurrection. This was the one doctrine through which the apostles filtered possible changes. Whether Jesus actually rose from the dead or not, it is certain that the one thing that the apostles constantly proclaimed was that He had risen. (See Acts 2:24; 2:32; 3:15; 3:26; 4:10; 5:30; 10:40.)

Why would the apostles use this as the very cornerstone of their creed if it was not well attested and firmly believed? They laid down their lives for this doctrine. Men do not lay down their lives for a doctrine that they do not firmly believe. They stated that they had seen Jesus after His resurrection, and rather than give up their statement, they died for it. Of course, men may die for error, and often have; however, in this case, the apostles knew whether they had seen Jesus or not. If they had not seen Jesus, they would not merely have been dying for error, but for a statement that they knew to be false. It is unbelievable that a person would do such a thing.

Furthermore, if the apostles firmly believed that Jesus rose from the dead, they had some facts on which they founded their belief. These are the facts they would have related in recounting the story; they would not have made up a story out of imaginary incidents. If the facts really happened as they are recounted in the Gospels, it is impossible to escape the conclusion that Jesus actually arose.

Furthermore, if Jesus had not risen, there would have been some evidence that He had not. His enemies would have found this evidence. But the apostles went up and down the very city where He had been crucified and proclaimed right to the face of the killers that He had been raised, and no one could produce evidence to the contrary. The best they could do was to say the guards went to sleep and the disciples stole the body while the guards slept. (See Matthew 28:12–13.) Men who bear evidence to what happens while they are asleep are hardly credible witnesses. Further still, if the apostles had stolen the body, they would have known it themselves, and they would not have been ready to die for what they knew to be a lie.

Another known fact is the change in the day of rest. The early church was first made up of Jews. For centuries, the Jews had celebrated the seventh day of the week as their day of rest and worship. But, we find the early Christians in the book of Acts, and also in early Christian writings, assembling on the first day of the week. (See Acts 20:7.)

Nothing is harder than to change a holy day that has been celebrated for centuries and is one of the most cherished customs of the people. What is especially significant about the change is that it came about not by a decree, but by general consent. Something tremendous must have happened that led to this change. The apostles asserted that what had happened on that day was the resurrection of Christ from the dead. That is the most rational explanation of the change; in fact, it is the only reasonable explanation.

But, the most significant fact of all is the change in the disciples—the moral transformation. At the time of the Crucifixion, we find the whole apostolic group filled with utter despair. We see Peter, the leader of the apostles, denying his Lord three times with oaths and curses. But, a few days later, we see this same man filled with a courage that nothing could shake. We see Peter standing before the very council that had condemned Jesus to death and saying to them,

> *Be it known unto you all, and to all the people of Israel, that by the name of Jesus Christ of Nazareth, whom ye crucified, whom God raised from the dead, even by him doth this man stand here before you whole.*   *(Acts 4:10)*

A little further on in this passage, when Peter and John are commanded by this council not to speak or teach at all in the name of Jesus, we hear them answering,

> *Whether it be right in the sight of God to hearken unto you more than unto God, judge ye. For we cannot but speak the things which we have seen and heard.*
> *(Acts 4:19–20)*

A little while later, the apostles are arrested and imprisoned, and they are in danger of death. The council sternly accuses them and commands them to be silent about Jesus. However, we hear Peter and the other apostles answering,

> *We ought to obey God rather than men. The God of our fathers raised up Jesus, whom ye slew and hanged on a tree. Him hath God exalted with his right hand to be a Prince and a Saviour....And we are his witnesses of these things.*   (Acts 5:29–32)

Something tremendous must have happened to account for this radical and astounding moral transformation. Nothing short of the fact of the Resurrection, of their having seen the risen Lord, will explain it.

These facts are so impressive and so conclusive that even infidel scholars and Jewish scholars have admitted that the apostles believed that Jesus rose from the dead. Even David Strauss said, "Only this much need be acknowledged, that the apostles firmly believed that Jesus had arisen." Strauss evidently did not wish to admit any more than he had to, but he felt compelled to admit that much. Schenkel went further yet and said,

It is an indisputable fact that in the early morning of the first day of the week following the crucifixion, the grave of Jesus was found empty. It is a second fact that the disciples and other members of the apostolic communion were convinced that Jesus was seen after the crucifixion.

These admissions are fatal to the rationalists who make them.

The question at once arises, "Where did the apostles get their conviction and belief that Jesus arose?" Renan attempted an answer by saying that "the passion of a hallucinated woman [Mary] gives to the world a resurrected God" (Renan's *Life of Jesus,* p. 357). By this, Renan suggested the following scenario: Mary was in love with Jesus. After His crucifixion, brooding over it, in the passion of her love, she had a hallucination of Jesus risen from the dead. She reported her dream as fact, and thus the passion of a hallucinating woman gave to the world a resurrected God.

But, we reply, the passion of a hallucinating woman was not enough to convince the world, or even the apostles. Remember the makeup of the apostolic group. In the apostolic group were a Matthew and a Thomas to be convinced, and outside the group was a Saul to be converted. The passion of a hallucinating woman could not convince a stubborn unbeliever like Thomas, or a Jewish tax collector like Matthew. Who ever heard of a tax collector, and, most of all, a Jewish tax collector, who could be influenced by the passion of a hallucinating woman? A hallucinating woman could not convince a fierce enemy like Saul of Tarsus either. We must find some saner explanation than this.

Strauss tried to account for the appearances of the resurrected Lord by saying that they might have been visions. To this we reply that, first of all, there was no reason for the apostles to have such visions. The apostles, far from expecting to see the Lord, scarcely believed their own eyes when they did see Him. (See Matthew 28:16–17; Luke 24:36–43.) Furthermore, who ever heard of eleven men having the same vision at the same time, to say nothing of five hundred men having the same vision at the same time? (See 1 Corinthians 15:6.) Strauss demanded that we give up one miracle and substitute five hundred miracles in its place. Nothing can surpass the gullibility of unbelief!

The third attempt at an explanation is that Jesus was not really dead when they took

Him down from the cross, that His friends nursed Him and brought Him back to life! According to this theory, the appearance of the risen Lord was really the appearance of one who had never been dead, but had only appeared to be dead and had merely been resuscitated. To support this view, it has been pointed out that Jesus hung only a short time on the cross. History tells us of a person in the time of Josephus who was taken down from the cross and nursed back to life.

To this we answer, first, that we must remember the events that preceded the Crucifixion: the agony in the Garden of Gethsemane (see Matthew 26:36–44), the awful ordeal of the four trials (see John 18:12–13, 24, 28–29; Luke 23:6–7), the scourging (see Matthew 27:26), and the consequent physical condition in which all this left Jesus. Remember, too, the water and the blood that poured from the pierced side. (See John 19:34.) Jesus' enemies took every precaution against Him being revived.

We reply, secondly, that if Jesus had been merely resuscitated, He would have been so weak, and such an utter physical wreck, that His reappearance would have been measured at its real value; and the moral transformation in the disciples, for which we are trying to account, would still remain unaccounted for. The officer in the time of Josephus who is cited as proof, though brought back to life, was an utter physical wreck.

We reply, in the third place, that the apostles and friends of Jesus, who are the ones who are supposed to have brought Him back to life, would have known how they brought Him back to life. They would have known that it was not a case of resurrection, but of resuscitation. And the main fact to be accounted for, namely, the change in them, would remain unaccounted for. The attempted explanation is an explanation that does not explain.

We reply, in the fourth place, that the moral difficulty is the greatest of all. If it was merely a case of resuscitation, then Jesus tried to pass Himself off as one risen from the dead when He was nothing of the sort. Then He was an utter impostor, and the whole Christian system rests on a fraud as its ultimate foundation. Is it possible to believe that such a system of religion as that of Christianity, embodying such exalted precepts and principles of truth, purity, and love, originated in a deliberately planned fraud? No one, except those whose own hearts are corrupted by fraud and trickery, can believe Jesus to have been an impostor and His religion to have been founded on fraud.

We have eliminated all other possible suppositions. We have but one left, namely, Jesus really was raised from the dead the third day as is recorded in the Gospels. Those who attempt to deny it are driven to desperate straits, which are further proof of the Resurrection.

We have, then, several independent lines of argument pointing decisively to the resurrection of Christ from the dead. Some of these taken separately prove the fact, but taken together they constitute an argument that makes it impossible for an open man to doubt the resurrection of Christ. Of course, if one is determined not to believe, no amount of proof will convince. Such a man must be left to his own deliberate choice of error and falsehood. But, any man who really desires to know the truth and is willing to obey it at any cost, must accept the resurrection of Christ as a historically proven fact.

There is really only one weighty objection to the doctrine that Christ rose from the dead, that is, that there is no conclusive evidence that anyone else ever arose. Here is a sufficient answer to this: Even if it were certain that no one else ever arose, it would not at all prove that Jesus did not rise. For the life of Jesus was unique. His nature was unique; His character was unique; His mission was unique; His history was unique. Therefore, it is not to be wondered at, but rather to be expected, that the conclusion of such a life should also be unique.

After all, this objection is simply a restatement of David Hume's argument against the possibility of the miraculous, an argument that has already been disproved. According to this argument, no amount of evidence can prove a miracle because miracles are contrary to all experience. But, are miracles contrary to *all* experience? To start out by saying that they are is to beg the very question at issue. They may be outside of your experience and mine; they may be outside the experience of this entire generation; but your experience and mine and the experience of this entire generation is not *all* experience. Every student of geology and astronomy knows that things have occurred in the past that are entirely outside the experience of the present generation. Things have occurred within the last four years that are entirely outside the experience of the fifty years preceding.

True science does not start out with a hypothesis that certain things are impossible. It simply studies the evidence to know what has actually occurred. It does not twist its observed facts to make them agree with predetermined theories, but seeks to make its theories agree with facts as observed. To say that miracles are impossible and that no amount of evidence can therefore prove a miracle, is to be supremely unscientific.

In the domain of chemistry, for example, discoveries have been made regarding radium that seemed to run counter to all previous observations regarding chemical elements and to well-established chemical theories. But, the scientist has not therefore said that these discoveries about radium cannot be true. Rather, he has gone to work to find out where the trouble was in his previous theories. The observed and recorded facts in the case before us prove that Jesus rose from the dead, and true science must accept this conclusion and conform its theories to this observed fact.

In the day of the great triumph of Deism in England, two of the most brilliant spokesmen for the denial of the supernatural were the eminent legal authorities, Gilbert West and Lord Lyttleton. These two men, who were put forward to crush the defenders of the supernatural events in the Bible, had a conference together. One of them said to the other that it would be difficult to maintain their position unless they disposed of two of the alleged bulwarks of Christianity, namely, the alleged resurrection of Jesus from the dead and the alleged conversion of Saul of Tarsus. Lyttleton said he would write a book to show that Saul of Tarsus was never converted as it is recorded in the Acts of the Apostles (see Acts 9:1–18), but that his alleged conversion was a myth. Gilbert West agreed to write another book to show that the alleged resurrection of Christ from the dead was a myth.

West said to Lyttleton, "I will have to depend on you for my facts, for I am somewhat rusty in my knowledge of the Bible." To this, Lyttleton replied that he was counting on West, for he too was somewhat rusty. One of them said to the other, "If we are to be honest in the matter, we ought to at least study the evidence," and this they undertook to do.

They had numerous conferences together while they were preparing their works. In one of these conferences, West said to Lyttleton that there had been something on his mind for some time that he thought he ought to discuss with him. He proceeded to say that as he had been studying the evidence, he was beginning to feel that there was something in it. Lyttleton replied that he was glad that he had told him this, for he himself had been somewhat shaken as he studied the evidence for the conversion of Saul of Tarsus.

Finally, when the books were finished and the two men met, West said to Lyttleton, "Have you written your book?" He replied that he had, but he said, "West, as I have been studying the evidence and weighing it by the recognized laws of legal evidence, I have been convinced that Saul of Tarsus was converted as stated in the Acts of the Apostles, and that Christianity is true, and I have written my book on that side." His book can be found today in top-notch libraries.

"Well," said West, "as I have studied the evidence for the resurrection of Jesus Christ from the dead, and have weighed it according to the acknowledged laws of evidence, I have been convinced that Jesus really rose from the dead as recorded in the Gospels, and I have written my book on that side." This book also can be found in our libraries today.

Let any lawyer, any man who is able to weigh evidence, yes, any man with average reasoning powers, and, above all, with perfect openness, study the facts regarding the Resurrection, and he will be convinced beyond a doubt that Jesus rose from the dead as recorded in the Gospels.

But, suppose He did rise from the dead; what of it? We will address that question in the next chapter.

8

What the Resurrection Proves

In the last three chapters, we have seen conclusive evidence that Jesus Christ rose from the dead. We have followed a number of independent lines of argument. Several of these taken alone satisfactorily prove the fact of the Resurrection, but taken together they constitute an argument that makes it impossible for a sincere man to doubt the Resurrection. But, suppose He did rise from the dead; what of it? What does His resurrection prove? It proves everything that needs to be proved the most. It proves everything that is essential to Christianity.

THERE IS A GOD

First of all, the resurrection of Christ from the dead proves that there is a God. It proves that the God of the Bible is the true God.

Every effect must have an adequate cause, and the only adequate cause that will account for the resurrection of Jesus Christ is God, the God of the Bible.

When Jesus was here on earth, He proclaimed the God of the Bible; the God of Abraham, Isaac, and Jacob; the God of the Old Testament as well as the New. He claimed that after men had put Him to death, the God of Abraham, Isaac, and Jacob, the God of the Bible, would raise Him from the dead the third day. (See Matthew 16:21.)

This was an astonishing claim to make, seemingly an absurd claim. For centuries men had come and gone. They had lived and died, and as far as human observation went, that was the end of them. But, Jesus claimed that after all these centuries of men living, dying, and passing into oblivion, that God, the God of the Bible, would raise Him from the dead.

Jesus died—He was crucified and buried. The appointed hour at which he had claimed God would raise Him from the dead came. God did raise Him from the dead, and thereby Jesus' astounding claim was substantiated. It was decisively proven that there is a God, and that the God of the Bible is the true God.

For centuries men have been seeking proofs of the existence and character of God.

There is the teleological argument, which is the argument of the marks of creative intelligence and design in the material universe—a good argument in its place. There is the argument of the intelligent guiding hand of God in human history; and there are other arguments, all more or less convincing. But, the resurrection of Jesus Christ from the dead provides us with a solid, scientific foundation for our faith in God.

In the light of the Resurrection, our faith in God is built on observed facts. In the light of the resurrection of Jesus, atheism and agnosticism no longer have any standing ground. It is no wonder that Peter said of Jesus, "By him [we] do believe in God, that raised him up from the dead, and gave him glory" (1 Pet. 1:21). My belief in the God of the Bible is not an uncertain whim. It is a fixed faith resting on an indisputably firm fact.

JESUS WAS SENT FROM GOD

In the second place, the resurrection of Jesus Christ from the dead proves that Jesus was a teacher sent from God. It proves that He received His message from God, that He was absolutely inerrant, and that He spoke the very words of God. These facts are what Jesus claimed about Himself. In John 7:16 He said, "My doctrine is not mine, but his that sent me." In John 12:49 He said, "I have not spoken of myself; but the Father which sent me, he gave me a commandment, what I should say, and what I should speak." In John 14:10–11 He said,

> *Believest thou not that I am in the Father, and the Father in me? the words that I speak unto you I speak not of myself: but the Father that dwelleth in me, he doeth the works. Believe me that I am in the Father, and the Father in me: or else believe me for the very works' sake.*

In John 14:24 He said, "The word which ye hear is not mine, but the Father's which sent me." His claim was that His words were the very words of God.

This, too, was an astonishing claim to make. Others have made similar claims; but the difference between their claims and Jesus' claim is that Jesus substantiated His claim, and no one else has ever substantiated his. God Himself unmistakably set His seal upon this astounding claim of Jesus Christ by raising Him from the dead.

In the light of the resurrection of Jesus Christ from the dead, how can a school of criticism assume to question the absolute inerrancy of Jesus Christ as a teacher, and set its authority up above that of Jesus? Such a school has absolutely no standing ground. Yes, that school of criticism, by putting forward its unsubstantiated claims in opposition to the demonstrated claims of Jesus Christ, makes itself a laughingstock in the eyes of thoughtful men.

JESUS IS THE SON OF GOD

In the third place, the resurrection of Jesus Christ from the dead proves that He is the Son of God. The apostle Paul said in Romans 1:4 that Jesus is "declared to be the Son of God with power...by the resurrection from the dead." And anyone who will stop to think will see that this is true beyond a doubt.

When Jesus was here on earth, He claimed to be divine in a sense in which no other man was divine. He taught that while even the greatest of God's prophets were only servants, He was a Son, an only Son. (See Mark 12:6; note the context.) He claimed that He and the Father were one (John 10:30), and that all men should honor Him, even as they honored the Father (John 5:23). He claimed that He was so completely and fully indwelt by God, was such a perfect and absolute incarnation of God, that whoever had seen Him had seen the Father

(John 14:9). This was a most amazing claim to make, a claim which, if not true, was the foulest blasphemy.

Jesus foretold to His enemies that they would put Him to death for making this claim, but that God Himself would set His seal to the claim by raising Him from the dead. Indeed, they did put Him to death for making this claim; those who disbelieved the deity of Jesus in that day caused Him to be nailed to the cross of Calvary for claiming to be divine. (See Matthew 26:63–66.) But, when the appointed hour had come, the breath of God swept through the dead body, and God Himself, as Jesus claimed He would, set His seal to Christ's assertion of His own deity by raising Him from the dead. God thus proclaimed to all ages, with clearer voice than if He should speak from the open heavens today, "This is My 'only begotten Son' (John 3:16), the One in whom I dwell in all My fullness (Col. 2:9), so that whoever has seen Him has seen the Father (John 14:9)." In the light of the Resurrection, belief systems that deny the deity of Jesus, such as Unitarianism, have absolutely no logical standing ground.

THERE WILL BE A JUDGMENT DAY

In the fourth place, the resurrection of Jesus Christ from the dead proves that there is a judgment day coming. On Mars Hill, Paul declared,

> [God] *hath appointed a day, in the which he will judge the world in righteousness by that man whom he hath ordained; whereof he hath given assurance unto all men, in that he hath raised him from the dead.* (Acts 17:31)

Thus, Paul made the resurrection of Christ the God-given assurance of the coming judgment.

But how does the resurrection of Christ give assurance of coming judgment? When Jesus was on earth, He declared that the Father had committed all judgment unto Him (John 5:22). He declared further that

> *The hour is coming, in the which all that are in the graves shall hear his voice, and shall come forth; they that have done good, unto the resurrection of life; and they that have done evil, unto the resurrection of damnation.*
> (John 5:28–29)

Men ridiculed His claim, hated Him for making the claim, put Him to death for making the claim (and for the other claim involved in it, that of deity), but God set His seal to the claim by raising Him from the dead.

The resurrection of Jesus Christ from the dead, which is an absolutely certain fact of history, points with an unerring finger to an absolutely certain judgment in the future. Belief in a coming judgment day is no guess of theologians. It is a positive faith founded on a profound fact. In the light of the resurrection of Jesus Christ from the dead, the man who continues in sin, flattering himself with the hope that there will be no future day of reckoning and of judgment, is guilty of madness. Jesus will sit in judgment, and every one of us must give account to Him of the deeds done in the body (2 Cor. 5:10).

BELIEVERS ARE JUSTIFIED

In the fifth place, the resurrection of Jesus Christ from the dead proves that every believer in Christ is justified from all things (Acts 13:39). We read in Romans 4:25 (RV) that Jesus "was delivered up for our trespasses, and was raised for our justification." More literally, He was delivered up because of our trespasses (that is, because we had trespassed), and was raised because of our justification (that is, because we were justified). The resurrection of

Jesus Christ proves decisively that the believer in Him is justified. But how?

When Jesus was on earth, He said that He would offer up His life as a ransom for many (Matt. 20:28). The hour came, and He offered up His life on the cross of Calvary as a ransom for us. Now, the atonement had been made, but there still remained a question: "Will God accept the atonement that has been offered?" For three nights and three days this question remained unanswered. Jesus lay in the grave, cold and dead. The long predicted hour came, the breath of God swept through that sleeping body, and Christ rose triumphant from the dead and was exalted to the right hand of the Father (Acts 2:32–33). Thus, God proclaimed to the whole universe, "I have accepted the atonement that Jesus made."

When Jesus died, He died as my representative, and I died in Him. (See Galatians 2:20.) When He arose, He arose as my representative, and I arose in Him. (See Romans 6:4.) When He ascended up on high and took His place at the right hand of the Father in glory, He ascended as my representative, and I ascended in Him. Today I am seated in Christ with God in heavenly places. (See Ephesians 2:6.)

I look at the cross of Christ, and I know that atonement has been made for my sins. I look at the open sepulcher and the risen and ascended Lord, and I know that the atonement has been accepted. There no longer remains a single sin on me (see Psalm 103:12), no matter how many or how great my sins may have been. My sins may have been as high as the mountains, but in the light of the Resurrection, the atonement that covers them is as high as the heavens. My sins may have been as deep as the ocean, but in the light of the Resurrection, the atonement that swallows them is as deep as eternity. In Acts 13:38–39 Paul declared,

> *Be it known unto you therefore, men and brethren, that through this man is preached unto you the forgiveness of sins: And by him all that believe are justified from all things.*

BELIEVERS WILL LIVE AGAIN

In the sixth place, the resurrection of Jesus Christ from the dead proves that all who are united to Christ by a living faith will live again. Paul said, "If we believe that Jesus died and rose again, even so them also which sleep in Jesus will God bring with him" (1 Thess. 4:14). The believer is so united to Christ by a living faith that if Christ rose, we must also rise. If the grave could not hold Him, it cannot hold us.

For centuries men have been seeking proofs of immortality; we have had the dreams of poets and the speculations of philosophers to cheer us with the hope that we will live again. But, even the best of philosophical arguments only point to the probability of a future life. In a matter like this, the human heart craves and demands something more than a probability.

In the resurrection of Jesus Christ from the dead, we get something more than probability—we get absolute certainty. We get scientific demonstration of life beyond the grave. The resurrection of Jesus Christ removes the hope of immortality from the domain of the speculative and the probable, and puts it into the domain of the scientifically demonstrated and certain. We know there is a life beyond the grave.

A popular preacher once said, "Many people are not at all sure that there is life beyond the grave. They wish it could be proven. So do I. But we can do no more than infer it from the moral constitution of the universe." I thank God that this popular preacher is wrong. Before the resurrection of Jesus Christ, perhaps, we could "do no more than infer it from the moral constitution of the universe." But, in the light of the Resurrection, it is no longer left to uncertain inferences from the moral constitution of the universe; it is proven! No further proof is needed. It is scientifically demonstrated. Anyone who candidly ponders the facts about the resurrection of Christ can never fail to believe and be certain that there is a future life.

In the light of Easter morning, I go out into the cemetery where lies the sleeping dust of my father, mother, brother, and child, and all my tears are brushed away, for I hear the Father saying, "Your father will live again; your mother will live again; your brother will live again; your child will live again."

BELIEVERS HAVE VICTORY OVER SIN

In the seventh place, the resurrection of Jesus Christ from the dead proves that it is the believer's privilege to have daily, hourly, constant victory over sin. We are united not only to the Lord who died to make atonement for our sin and to deliver us from the guilt of sin; we are united to the Lord who rose again, who "ever liveth to make intercession for [us]," and who has power "to save [us] to the uttermost" (Heb. 7:25), power to keep us from falling day by day, and "to present [us] faultless before the presence of his glory with exceeding joy" (Jude 1:24). I may be weak, utterly weak, unable to resist temptation for a single hour; but He is strong, infinitely strong, and He lives to give me help and deliverance every day and every hour.

The question of victory over sin is not a question of my weakness, but of His strength, His resurrection power, always at my disposal. He has all power in heaven and on earth (Matt. 28:18), and what my risen Lord has, belongs to me also. In the light of the resurrection of Jesus Christ from the dead, failure in daily living is unnecessary and inexcusable. In His resurrection life and power, it is our privilege and our duty to lead victorious lives.

Four men were once climbing up the slippery side of the Matterhorn: a guide and a tourist, a second guide and a second tourist, all roped together. The lower tourist lost his footing and went over the side. The sudden pull on the rope carried the lower guide with him, and he carried the other tourist with him. Three men were now dangling over the lofty cliff. But the guide who was in the lead, feeling the first pull on the rope, drove his pike into the ice, braced his feet, and held fast. Three men dangling over the awful abyss, but three men safe, because they were tied to the man who held fast. The first tourist regained his place on the path, the guide regained his, and the lower tourist regained his. On and up they went in safety.

As the human race ascended the icy cliffs of life, the first Adam lost his footing and swept over the abyss. He pulled the next man after him, and the next, and the next, and the next, until the whole race hung over the abyss. But, the Second Adam, the Man in glory, stood fast; and all who are united to Him by a living faith, though dangling over the awful precipice, are safe, because they are tied to the Man in glory.

9

The Causes of Unbelief

The profession of unbelief is very common in our day. (When I speak of unbelief, I am referring to unbelief in Christ and the Bible.) I am constantly meeting with those who tell me that the reason they are not Christians is that they do not believe in the Bible. There are many preachers, most excellent and gifted men, who think that unbelief is not worthy of attention, that the proper way to treat it is to ignore it.

I do not agree with them. Unbelief is common enough, active enough, and destructive enough, to demand attention. While I do not for a moment think that the cause of Christ or the Bible has anything to fear from unbelief, I do know that individuals and communities are being greatly injured by it; and we owe it to them to expose its real character, to point out its consequences, and to show its cure.

I have had no greater joy now for some years than to be able to lead many men out of the confusion and wretchedness of unbelief into the clear light and abounding joy of an intelligent faith in Christ and the Bible.

MISREPRESENTATIONS OF CHRISTIANITY

What are the causes of unbelief? The first cause, and one of the commonest, is misrepresentation of Christianity by its professed disciples. There are two kinds of misrepresentations: first, misrepresentations in doctrine; and second, misrepresentations in daily living. Let us look first at the misrepresentations in doctrine.

Take, for example, what has been preached as Christianity for generations in France, Spain, Italy, the Philippine Islands, Mexico, and the South American republics. Of course, *we* know that this is only the grossest distortion of the Christianity of the Bible, but the common people of these lands do not know this. They suppose that the Christianity preached by the priests is the Christianity of the Bible. Is it any wonder that they reject it and become out-and-out infidels? If what is thus preached as Christianity were Christianity, I would reject Christianity myself.

But, many so-called Protestant representations of Christianity, if not so grossly false, are still false. There is a wide difference between the God of the Bible and the God of much so-called Protestant teaching, between the Christ of the Bible and the Christ of much so-called Protestant teaching, and between the Christian life as set forth in the Bible and the ethics set forth in much so-called Protestant teaching.

However, the grossest misrepresentations of Christianity on the part of its professed disciples are the misrepresentations in daily living. The lives of many professed Christians are so widely at variance with the life taught in the Bible that they lead many observers into utter unbelief. Take, for example, the professed Christian who oppresses his employees in their wages. How many a professed Christian employer there is today who overworks his employees almost beyond endurance. Is it any wonder that these employees say that they have no use for Christianity?

Look at the professed Christians in business who are dishonest in trade, who misrepresent their products, who use all kinds of dishonorable means to get ahead of their competitors in business. Is it any wonder that people looking on are led to give up Christianity thus misrepresented?

On one occasion, I attended the wedding of a young businessman in the city of Chicago. After the ceremony I began to speak to him about becoming a Christian, but he replied, "You do not need to talk to me about that. I work for ———— Company. The owners are very prominent in the church, but I know how they carry on their business. I have no desire to be a Christian."

Look at the professed Christian who stores up his millions and lives in lavish luxury while the poor are starving at his doors. You may say to me that these misrepresentations of Christianity are no sufficient excuse for unbelief, that men and women ought to learn to distinguish between real Christianity and its counterfeit, and this I admit. A really intelligent man never refuses good money because there is counterfeit money in circulation. But many men do not distinguish. They do not read the Bible for themselves, and their only idea of Christianity is from what they see in the lives and teachings of its professed disciples. Then they say, "If that is Christianity, I do not want it." So, they become infidels.

One of the most noted infidels of modern times claimed that it was the inconsistent living of his own father, who was a Baptist preacher, that first led him into unbelief. Whether his picture of his father's character was true or not, or whether he grossly misrepresented his father to defend his own unbelief, as I have heard it alleged that he did, I cannot say. But, this I do know, that beyond a question, in many instances, the inconsistencies of professedly Christian parents have led their children into utter unbelief.

Misrepresentation of Christianity by its professed disciples in their teachings, and especially in their lives, has done more to manufacture infidels than all the writings and speeches of all the Paines and Voltaires and Ingersolls of the world.

IGNORANCE

The second cause of unbelief is ignorance— ignorance of what the Bible contains and teaches, ignorance of history, and ignorance of true science. The average infidel knows almost nothing about the Bible. He has caught a few difficulties here and there from the writings or speeches of other infidels, but of the real contents of the Bible, he knows practically nothing.

I once asked a man if he would become a Christian. He replied, "No, I am an infidel."

"Why are you an infidel?" I asked.

"Because the Bible is full of contradictions," he replied.

"Well," I said, "if the Bible is full of contradictions, please show me one."

"Why," he said, "it is full of them."

"If it is full of them, you ought be able to show me at least one."

"Why, it is full of them."

"Well, show me one."

"Well, it is in the book of Psalms." I handed him my Bible to find it, and he began looking for the Psalms in the back part of the New Testament.

"Let me find the book of Psalms for you." When I found the Psalms for him, he began to fumble around for awhile; then he said, "If I had my Bible here I could show it to you."

"Will you bring your Bible tonight and meet me here at the close of the meeting?" He promised that he would. The appointed hour came, and I was at the appointed place, but my infidel friend did not appear. I had taken the precaution of getting his address, and I went to the address he had given. I found it was an inn, but I did not find my man. Months afterwards, after one of our meetings, one of my students called to me and said, "Come here. Here is a man who says the Bible is full of contradictions." I went over, and behold, it was the same man! The man evidently thought I would not recognize him, but I did, and I said, "You are the man who lied to me."

He dropped his head and said, "Yes."

Another smart, young infidel once said to me, "I don't believe the Bible." I asked him why not. He replied, "I don't believe that passage that speaks about Christ calling down fire from heaven to destroy His enemies." When I assured him that there was no such passage in the Bible, he would not believe me.

An infidel in Edinburgh asked me to explain the passage that said, "Cain went into the land of Nod and *took to himself* a wife." When I said the Bible does not say so, he offered to bet me a hundred pounds that it did.

Colonel Ingersoll, the high priest of the cheaper and more superficial unbelief of the day, is an illustration of this ignorance of the Bible. He said in one of his lectures, "There is not a single kind and loving sentiment attributed to Christ that was not uttered by Buddha at least five hundred years before Christ was born." I would like to know where he finds any utterance of Buddha similar to John 13:34: "A new commandment I give unto you, That ye love one another; as I have loved you, that ye also love one another." Or, John 15:12–13:

> *This is my commandment, That ye love one another, as I have loved you. Greater love hath no man than this, that a man lay down his life for his friends.*

Or, Matthew 20:28: "Even as the Son of man came not to be ministered unto, but to minister, and to give his life a ransom for many."

In another place, Colonel Ingersoll said, "If Christ ever lived on the earth, He was an infidel in His time." I would like to know what Colonel Ingersoll does with passages in which Jesus affirms his belief in the Scriptures, such as John 10:35: "The scripture cannot be broken." Or, Matthew 5:18: "Till heaven and earth pass, one jot or one tittle shall in no wise pass from the law, till all be fulfilled." Or, Mark 7:13, where, speaking of the law of Moses, He calls it "the word of God." Or, Luke 24:27, 44:

> *And beginning at Moses and all the prophets, he expounded unto them in all the scriptures the things concerning himself....And he said unto them, These are the words which I spake unto you, while I was yet with you, that all things*

*must be fulfilled, which were written in
the law of Moses, and in the prophets,
and in the psalms, concerning me.*

If this is unbelief, then I am an unbeliever. But
all intelligent men know this is not unbelief,
and that Colonel Ingersoll was simply parading
his ignorance when he uttered his statement.

Some years ago, one of the English leaders
of unbelief wrote an article in one of the anti-
Christian journals in which he spoke of Matthew as a "dispenser of liquors." He knew so
little of the Bible that he supposed the word
publican used of Matthew in the Bible (Matt.
10:3) meant publican in the sense of a saloon-
keeper.

In Germany, the most prominent spokes-
man for materialistic anti-Christianity is so
ignorant of the historic discussions of Christian doctrine that he speaks of the virgin birth
of our Lord as "the Immaculate Conception."
One of the most prominent spokesmen of anti-
Christianity in England does the same thing.

CONCEIT

The third cause of unbelief is conceit.
Many men tell us that they are infidels because
they find things in the Bible that they cannot
understand, and because the Bible has apparent

contradictions that they cannot reconcile. To say that a thing cannot be true because I cannot understand it, to think that God could not utter anything that would be beyond my understanding, is the highest conceit. It is to assume that I know all things, that I know as much as God knows, and that therefore God could not possibly utter anything that I could not understand. To think that because I cannot find the solution of a difficulty that therefore none can be found, is to think that I know all things, or that my mind is infinite; it is to think that I am God.

Suppose I should take my little child outside around sunset and say to the child, "Do you see the sun over there?" "Yes." "Well, my child, that sun is over ninety-two million miles away." Then suppose the child should look up into my face in her mature wisdom of nine years and say, "Father, I know that is not true. The sun is just behind the barn over there." Would this be a revelation of the child's wisdom, or of her ignorance and conceit? The oldest, wisest philosopher compared with the Infinite is less than a child compared with the wisest man.

Likewise, for us to challenge our Father's statements because they seem untrue to us, does not reveal us to be philosophers worthy of admiration and applause, but to be foolish children who ought to be sent to bed. If we find difficulties in the Bible that we cannot explain, a little modesty on our part would lead us to say, "If I knew a little more, I might be able to readily explain this difficulty," rather than to say, "This Book that contains a difficulty that I cannot explain surely cannot be from God."

When I was in Birmingham, a man who parades his unbelief by having quotations from various infidels at the top of his stationery, wrote me saying that the Bible could not be the Word of God because it is full of contradictions. He claimed that he could send me hundreds of them, but that one or two would suffice, because they could not be answered. The difficulties he sent had very simple solutions, and I wrote him the solutions. However, instead of rethinking his conviction that the difficulties he held were insoluble, he wrote that he was sorry that he had been so unfortunate in his choice of difficulties before, but would now send me some more. These were just as easily solved. But, he still did not seem to believe that his other apparently unanswerable difficulties would be as easy to solve as these formerly unanswerable difficulties, if he only knew a little more.

SIN

The fourth cause of unbelief is sin. This is the most common and most fundamental cause of unbelief. Sin causes unbelief in two ways. First, men sin and then embrace unbelief to find comfort in their sin. There is no book that makes men so uneasy in their sin as the Bible, and if they can only make themselves believe that the Bible is not true, it gives them some solace in the pursuit of sin. Men tell you that they have many objections to the Bible; but with the majority of them, their greatest objection to the Bible, if they would confess the truth to themselves and to others, is that it condemns their sin, and makes them uneasy in their sin.

Second, sin blinds men's eyes to the truth of the Bible, and makes it appear as foolishness. There is nothing that blinds the mind to truth the way sin does. I was once called to deal with an infidel. I sat down, and he told me that the reason that he could not be a Christian was a difficulty he had with the Bible. I asked him what his difficulty was. He replied that he could not see where Cain got his wife. I said, "Will you come to Christ if I tell you where Cain got his wife?"

"Oh," he said, "I will not promise that."

"But," I said, "if that is the difficulty that keeps you from coming to Christ, and if you are an honest man and I remove that difficulty, you will come to Christ."

"No, I will not promise that."

I then went to the root of the matter. I found out that his real difficulty was not about Cain's wife at all, but about another man's wife. It is surprising how often young men who fall into sin and into loose ways of living fall also into unbelief.

My former colleague, Professor W. W. White, was speaking one time in Chicago on "The Mistakes of Ingersoll." At the close of the lecture, a fine-looking man approached him and said, "Professor White, you have no right to say what you have said today, that you are a Christian and I am an infidel. I have just as much right to my opinion as you have to yours."

Professor White then asked him a pointed question: "Is your life pure?"

The man replied, "That is none of your business. My life is just as pure as yours is." Then Professor White asked him his name. The man said, "That is none of your business."

"But," said Professor White, "I want to look up your record." The man declined to give his name, and began to back out of the hall.

But, some people that were gathered around knew the man's name, and they gave it to Professor White.

Within two years from that time, that man was found dead in a Boston hotel, side by side with a young woman, not his wife, whom he had beguiled into unbelief, and who had gone off with him to lecture on anti-Christianity. They were found dead together in this Boston hotel, with the gas turned on.

Dear readers, my statement that sin causes unbelief will make some of you angry, but look into your own hearts and lives and see if there is not some sin at the root of your unbelief. I do not say that all unbelief comes from sin, but I do say, after long and careful observation, that a very large share of the current unbelief of the day has sin for its ultimate cause.

RESISTANCE TO THE HOLY SPIRIT

The fifth cause of unbelief is resistance to the Holy Spirit. This is a very common cause of unbelief. The Spirit of God moves upon the hearts of men, inclining them to accept Christ. They will not yield to the Spirit of God. They resist the Holy Spirit, and the light that He gives to the soul is darkened, and they fall into skepticism or unbelief.

In one of my pastorates, there was a lawyer of excellent abilities who was a most bitter opponent of Christianity. He did what he could to oppose Christianity by bringing infidel lecturers to the town. I looked into this man's history. I found that there was a time in the very church of which I was pastor when he was under conviction of sin, and hesitating as to whether he should come and accept Christ. And, when pressed about the subject, he replied, "No, I cannot be a Christian and succeed in my business, and I must support my family."

The light that was dawning on his soul went out, and darkness and unbelief settled down upon him, exercising such a blighting influence over his life that he lost the confidence of his fellowmen and lost his law practice. Last I knew, his wife was teaching school to help support the family, while he was doing whatever odd jobs he could get.

In one of the western colleges, there was a revival of religion. Two young men in the college set themselves against it. They were determined not to yield. They made an agreement together to meet on a certain evening and go into the chapel and blaspheme the Holy Spirit. They met at the appointed hour, but the heart of one of the young men failed him, and he was afterwards converted. The other went into the college chapel alone. What he did in there no one knows, but he came out white as a sheet. He drifted in unbelief, and became a leader in one of the secular societies in one of our large cities.

Oh, those of you who are resisting the Holy Spirit, if I could visit you five years from now, I would most likely find you an infidel. And if I come back ten years from now, in all probability I would find you a drunkard. In the city of Melbourne, more than one man came to me, a moral wreck, who said that his fall was due to the influence of the noted infidel in that place.

In the next chapter we will examine the consequences and cure of unbelief.

10

Unbelief: Its Consequences and Cure

In the last chapter, we saw the causes of unbelief: first, misrepresentations of Christianity on the part of its professed adherents; second, ignorance of the Bible, and of history, and of science; third, conceit; fourth, sin; and fifth, resistance to the Holy Spirit. In this chapter, we will discuss the consequences and cure of unbelief.

CONSEQUENCES OF UNBELIEF

Sin

The first consequence of unbelief is sin. Unbelief breeds sin; there is no doubt about that. It is caused by sin, and in turn it produces a progeny like its ancestry. Sin first entered into human history through questioning God's Word. When the Devil sought to lead Eve into disobedience to God, he began by insinuating that the Word of God was not true. He first said, "Hath God said" (Gen. 3:1), and then he flatly denied what God had said. The Devil was the first infidel lecturer. He had an audience of only one, but he reached millions through that lecture. He saw at once how effective this mode of attack is on man's moral integrity.

From that day to this, the Devil has been trapping men into sin by sowing the seeds of unbelief in their hearts. He well knows what sort of a crop that seed brings forth. When a young person falls into unbelief, look out for his morals. Unbelief forms a very rickety foundation for an upright character.

A former president of the British National Secular Society, Joseph Barker, who, in fact, was elected to Parliament, said, "I have seen the dreadful effects that unbelief produces on men's characters; I have had proof of its deteriorating effects in my own experience; its tendency is to utter debasement." Occupying the position that he did, Joseph Barker certainly knew unbelief and knew its consequences, and his testimony to its destructive effects on character is true beyond question.

Anarchy

The second consequence of unbelief is anarchy. Anarchists are, of necessity, always infidels. It is impossible for a man who believes in the Bible to be an anarchist. When Vaillant, the miserable French vagabond and anarchist, stood on the gallows, he boasted of his unbelief. His unbelief and his anarchy went hand in hand. Louis Blanc, one of the great leaders of anarchy, is reported to have said, "When I was an infant, I rebelled against my nurse; when I was a child, I rebelled against my tutors and my parents; when I was a man, I rebelled against the government; when I die, if there is any heaven and I go there, I will rebel against God."

The acceptance of Christianity would do away with anarchy on the one hand, and it would do away with the oppression of the poor by the rich that leads to anarchy on the other hand.

Despair

The third consequence of unbelief is wretchedness and despair. God has created us for fullness of joy, and has made fullness of joy possible for each one of us. (See Psalm 16:11.)

But, fullness of joy such as God intends for man, and which alone can satisfy a soul made in God's image, can only come from a living faith in Jesus as the Son of God, and in the Bible as the Word of God. Infidels are never profoundly happy. They may have surface happiness, but it is not, as everyone knows who knows them well, deep and satisfying.

One night as I closed a lecture in a New Zealand town, a middle-aged man passed in front of the platform as he made his way out of the building. He looked up at me and scowled and said, "I am an infidel." I replied, "You do not need to tell us that; your face shows it. You are one of the most miserable-looking men I have ever seen." I received a letter from him the next day saying that he *was* miserable.

Have you ever known a joyous, old infidel? Happy they may be, at least at times when in company, but did you ever see that deep, continuous, overflowing joyfulness that is so characteristic of the aged Christian?

On the day of the death of a noted American infidel, I was with a friend of his, and we got to talking about him. He said to me, "Lately, every time I had gone to see him, his wife said to me, 'Don't tell him that he is growing old; it makes him very angry.'" But, it does not make the aged Christian angry to tell him he is growing old, for he knows he is only ripening for a better world.

Unbelief very often produces despair and suicide. Even the best of pagan writers taught the propriety of suicide. For example, Epictetus said, "The door is open. When you will, you can leave off playing the game of life." On the other hand, Mrs. Amelia E. Barr, who has studied suicide, said, "The advent of Christianity made self-destruction a crime." She further said that the infidel revival in France at the time of the Revolution caused the abolition of the civil and canon laws against suicide. She further said, "The great underlying cause of the advance of modern suicide is the advance of lax or skeptical religious views."

Unbelief logically leads to pessimism and despair. Ingersoll himself wrote an editorial in a New York newspaper in defense of suicide. After it was published, New York and the surrounding area had a harvest of suicides. The man who wrote the editorial was directly responsible for its consequences, and it is no wonder that the editorial raised a storm of protest and indignation. But, his article was the logical outcome of his unbelief.

There came to Chicago, at the time of the World's Fair, a poor but brilliant young woman from one of the southern states. Her intellectual gifts were so great that she was introduced into the best society, where she spoke on "The New Woman." She was led into anti-Christianity by an able advocate of unbelief in Chicago, but her career as an infidel was brief. She soon met a suicide's death in an eastern city, and one branch of the infidels of America meets annually at her grave to commemorate her death. Her brokenhearted father also died by his own hand. Such is the legitimate fruit of unbelief.

A Hopeless Grave

The fourth consequence of unbelief is a hopeless grave. Colonel Ingersoll once said, "The pulpit has cast a shadow over the cradle and a gloom over the grave." If this is true, it is a most remarkable fact that people, even professedly infidel people, are so anxious to have Christian preachers conduct their funerals. There is a gloom over the grave by nature and by sin, but the Bible dispels the shadow. Throw away the Bible, and you do not get rid of the gloom; however, you do get rid of the light that illuminates it. Unbelief shrouds the grave in gloom, and the only rays of light are those stolen from Christianity.

Colonel Ingersoll, at his brother's grave, delivered an address, eloquent in words, but sad beyond description. As he drew towards the close of that address, he said that through the darkness, hope sees the glimmering of a star; but he was not honest enough to say that that star was the Star of Bethlehem.

On the other hand, D. L. Moody, at his brother's grave, sounded forth a note of joy and exultation. Looking into the grave, he cried,

> *O death, where is thy sting? O grave, where is thy victory? The sting of death is sin; and the strength of sin is the law. But thanks be to God, which giveth us the victory through our Lord Jesus Christ.*   *(1 Cor. 15:55–57)*

These two men died the same year in America, Colonel Ingersoll, the acknowledged leader of American unbelief, and D. L. Moody, the leader of Christian activity. Compare the deaths and funerals of these two men, and see for yourselves whether the Christian's death or the infidel's is the gloomy one.

The death of Colonel Ingersoll was sudden, and without a ray of cheer and brightness; his funeral was inexpressibly pitiful. His wife and daughter, who loved him, could not bear to have the body taken from the house until the beginning of decay made it an absolute necessity. It was all they had, and despairingly they clung to that body, now decaying. The scene at the crematory, as described in the daily papers, was enough to make the heart of anyone ache, no matter how little one might be in sympathy with the views of the unfortunate man who passed into eternity.

On the other hand, the death and funeral of Mr. Moody were triumphant in every detail. Early on the morning of his departure from this world, his eldest son was sitting beside his bed. He heard his father speaking in a low tone of voice, and as he leaned over to listen, these were the words that he heard: "Earth is receding; heaven is opening; God is calling."

"You are dreaming, Father," said the son.

"No, Will, this is no dream. I have been within the gates. I have seen the children's faces."

The family were summoned. Mr. Moody rallied. A while later, he began to sink again, and he was heard to say, "Is this death? This is not bad; there is no valley. This is bliss. This is glorious."

"Father," said his daughter, "you must not leave us. We cannot spare you."

The dying man replied, "I am not going to throw my life away if God has any more work for me to do; I will get well and do it. But if God is calling, I must be up and off."

He rallied again. He gained sufficient strength to rise from the bed and walk over to the window, and he sat down in a chair and talked with his family. He began to think he would recover, and was contemplating sending for his pastor to pray for his recovery; but beginning to sink again, he asked them to help him back to the bed. As he was sinking, his daughter knelt by the bed and started to pray for his recovery, but he said, "No, no, Emma, don't pray that. God is calling. This is my coronation day. I have been looking forward to it"; and the heroic warrior was swept up into the presence of the King.

At the funeral, all was triumphant. His son said to me before the service, "Remember, there is to be nothing of sadness in the service. We want nothing but triumph here today." The body was borne to the church by students from one of the schools that he had founded. It lay in an open casket in front of the pulpit. Right in front of it, with unveiled faces, sat his wife and daughter and sons, listening with peaceful faces to the words that were spoken, and joining in the hymns of gladness and praise and victory. When others were done speaking, the eldest son rose and gladly gave a testimony about his father and the power of his faith.

Is it Christianity that throws a gloom over the grave? Is the Christian's grave the gloomy one, and the infidel's the bright one? Who ever heard of a Christian repenting on his deathbed that he had been a Christian? It is not at all uncommon for infidels to repent on their deathbeds that they have been infidels.

Eternal Ruin

The fifth consequence of unbelief is eternal ruin. We are told in Mark 16:16, "He that believeth and is baptized shall be saved; but he that believeth not shall be damned." We are told in John 3:36, "He that believeth on the Son hath everlasting life: and he that believeth not the Son shall not see life; but the wrath of God abideth on him."

We have all sinned (Rom. 3:23), but the only way to find pardon is by the acceptance of the Sin-bearer whom God has provided. If we prefer to be infidels and reject Him, there is no hope. Jesus is the only Savior who has ever proved competent to save men from the power of sin here, so we may rest assured He is the only One who will prove competent to save men from the consequences of sin hereafter.

There are many who do not profess to be infidels who are not theoretically so, but are practically so. All who reject Christ are infidels in practice, and they will be lost.

As Ethan Allen, a brave soldier but a hopeless infidel, stood at his daughter's death-bed, she turned to him and asked whether she should accept his unbelief or her mother's faith, and the humbled man advised her to accept her mother's faith in that trying hour.

THE CURE FOR UNBELIEF

Christian Living

We come now to the cure for unbelief. The great cure for unbelief is Christian living on the part of professed Christians. There is no argument for Christianity like a Christlike life. Many a skeptic and infidel has been won by the life of one who not merely believed in Christ intellectually, but who lived like Him in his daily walk.

McAll lay dead in his coffin in Paris. A workman of Paris, a former anarchist, stood by his coffin weeping. "Was he a relative?" someone asked.

"No," he replied.

"Why, then, do you weep?"

"He saved me."

"What did he say?"

"He said nothing," replied the former anarchist. "It was his face." The Christlike character shining out in a Christlike countenance had saved this man.

I was once asked to call on a woman of brilliant gifts who was an unbeliever. "There is one thing I cannot get around," she said, "and that is my father's life." Not long afterwards, by the power of the truth that was exemplified in her father's life, which lead her to a deeper study of the Bible, she became an openly professed follower of Jesus Christ.

A Surrendered Will

In the second place, the cure for unbelief is a surrendered will on the part of the infidel. Jesus said, "If any man willeth to do [God's] will, he shall know of the teaching, whether it be of God, or whether I speak from myself" (John 7:17 RV). Any man afflicted with the malady of skepticism can find a remedy, if he wants it, in this simple prescription. Nothing so clarifies a person's spiritual vision as a surrendered will. By this simple act of the surrender of the will to God, many a man has found the mists of his unbelief scattered in a moment.

When I was in New Zealand, a well-known and well-educated commercial traveler came to me and said, "My friends want me to speak to you. I am an agnostic, but I know that you cannot help me." I told him that I thought I could, but he was sure that I could not.

"What do you believe?" I asked.

"I don't know that I believe anything."

"Do you not believe that there is an absolute difference between right and wrong?"

"Yes, I do."

"Will you take your stand upon the right to follow it wherever it carries you?"

"I think I am doing that now."

"Will you definitely here today take your stand upon the right to follow it wherever it carries you, no matter what it costs?"

He said, "I will."

Then I went over the same ground and practically the same propositions as I did in my talk with the agnostic in Chicago, which I wrote about in the fourth chapter. This man also agreed to everything but assured me that nothing would come of it. Some weeks later in Dunedin, this man's wife came to me and said, "I have had a letter from my husband that I do not understand. He said I may show it to you." In the letter he said that he thought he was converted, but that he was not quite sure yet. He said that she could show this letter to me and to the minister, but not to anyone else until he was perfectly sure of his position. He afterwards made a full profession of his faith in the Bible and in Christ.

The Study of God's Word

The third part of the cure for unbelief is the study of the Word of God. Men do not need to study books of Christian evidences. The Bible is its own best proof. Let any real seeker of the truth, anyone who sincerely desires to know the truth and is willing to obey it whatever it costs, get down to the earnest study of the Bible, and he will soon become convinced that it is the Word of God.

In my first pastorate, there was a member of my church who had a brother who was a lecturer on scientific subjects; however, this lecturer was an infidel. Sometimes he would lecture on the contradictions between science and the Bible. She came to me and asked if I would pray for him that he might be converted. This I agreed to do. Some time after this, she came to me and said that her brother had written her a letter, saying that he had become a Christian. In this letter he gave her the reason for his conversion. It was this: "I have recently been studying the Bible, and have become convinced that it is the Word of God." It would have been better if he had studied the Bible before he lectured on it, and the contradictions between it and science.

In one of my pastorates, I had a friend who lived across the street from me who was an agnostic. Though he was an agnostic, and I a Christian minister, we were close friends, for I believe that Christians, and Christian ministers, should associate with all classes of men. I do not believe at all in the division of society into men, women, and ministers. I think a minister should be a man among men. How can we expect to influence men unless we touch elbows with them? Our Master was not too good to associate with all kinds and conditions of men, even the most depraved and outcast. (See Matthew 9:11.) Should we think ourselves better than our Master?

I read in my Bible that Christians are "the salt of the earth" (Matt. 5:13). How on earth can we expect the salt to exert its preservative influence on the meat if we put the salt in one barrel and the meat in another? So I have always cultivated the friendship, not merely of orthodox Christians, but of all kinds of "heretics" and unbelievers.

This man and I were good friends. We often met and talked together. One night we were standing together on his front lawn just as the sun went down, when he suddenly said, "Mr. Torrey, I am sixty-six years of age. I cannot live many more years. I have no one to leave my money to, and I cannot take it with me. I would give every penny of it if I could believe as you do."

I replied, "That is very easy. I can tell you how."

We went into the house, and I asked his wife for a sheet of paper, and I wrote on it the following words: "I believe that there is an absolute difference between right and wrong." (I did not say I believe that there is a God, for this man was an agnostic, neither affirming nor denying the existence of God, and you have to begin where a man is.) "And I hereby take my stand upon the right to follow it wherever it carries me. I promise to make an honest search to find out if Jesus Christ is the Son of God; and if I find out that He is, I promise to accept Him as my Savior, and to confess Him as such before the world."

Having written this out, I handed it to my friend and said, "Will you sign that?" He replied, "Why, anybody ought to be willing to sign that. You only ask me to agree to do what my own conscience tells me I ought to do. Anybody ought to be willing to sign that."

"Will you sign it?" I asked.

"Why," he added more earnestly, "anybody ought to be willing to sign that."

I said, "Will you sign it?"

Still more earnestly he said, "Anybody ought to be willing to sign it."

"Will *you* sign it?"

"I will think about it," he said. He never signed it. He died as he had lived, without God, without Christ, without hope. He went out into the darkness of a Christless eternity. He told the truth about one thing. He did not take one penny of his money with him. They laid him in a Christless grave. He is now in a Christless eternity. But whose fault was it? He was shown a way out of darkness into light, a way that he admitted his own conscience told him to take, and he would not take it.

Reader, the same way has been shown to you. Follow it, and it will lead you as it has thousands of others, out of the uncertainty, restlessness, and ultimate despair of unbelief, into the certainty, the joy, the victory, and the ultimate glory of an intelligent faith in the Bible as the Word of God, and in Christ as the Son of God.